M017698

P9-CDV-426

85-312
017698

HQ
759      Gansberg, Judith M.
G36           The second nine months
1984

GARLAND COUNTY
COMMUNITY COLLEGE
LIBRARY
Hot Springs, ARkansas  71913

86-3/2

direct  10/18/85

12.95

# THE SECOND NINE MONTHS

# THE SECOND NINE MONTHS

by

Judith M. Gansberg
and
Arthur P. Mostel, M.D.

GARLAND COUNTY
COMMUNITY COLLEGE
LIBRARY
Hot Springs, AR 71901

College of the Ouachitas

TRiBECA
COMMUNICATIONS, INC.
New York, N.Y.

Copyright © 1984 Judith M. Gansberg and Arthur P. Mostel

All rights reserved. No part of this book may be reproduced or utilized in any form, or by any means, electronic or mechanical, including photocopying, recording, or by any information storage or retrieval system, without permission in writing from the Publisher. Inquiries should be addressed to Tribeca Communications, Inc., 401 Broadway, New York, New York 10013.

**Library of Congress Cataloging in Publication Data**

Gansberg, Judith M.
    The second nine months.

    Bibliography: p.
    1. Mothers—Psychology.  2. Mothers—Sexual behavior.  3. Puerperium—Psychological aspects.  4. Marriage—Psychological aspects.  I. Mostel, Arthur P., 1934-    II. Title.
HQ759.G36    1984           155.6'463          83-24323
ISBN 0-943392-45-4


Distributed in Canada by Prentice-Hall Canada Inc., 1870 Birchmount Road, Scarborough, Ontario M1P 2J7

Printed in the United States of America
First Edition:  February 1984

1   2   3   4   5   6   7   8   9   10

HQ
759
G 36
1984
# Dedication

To Judy's daughter, Brianne, without whom this book would never have come to be, and

To Arthur's wife, Stella and children Robert, Carolyn and Linda, who taught him how to be a husband and father, and to his father, William, who shared his dream of being a doctor with him.

# Acknowledgments

We wish to thank all the women who allowed us to interview them for this book. Without their openness and honesty, we could not have completed our task.

Thanks are also due to a number of professionals who contributed their knowledge, advice and experience to our efforts. Their help was much appreciated. They are Carol Cederbaum, A.C.S.W.; Lorraine Ebel, M.S., C.C.T.; Carol Mann-Cohen, A.C.S.W.; Stella Mostel, M.S., A.C.S.T.; and Dr. Richard Lee Zimmern.

We must also thank Judy's husband, Bob Burger, whose patience and abilities in child care created the time and atmosphere for our work.

J.M.G.
A.P.M.
Stamford, Ct.

# Contents

CHAPTER ONE
# To Tell It Like It Is

*"There is something about your own child," said Brooke. "That love . . . you don't even realize it yourself immediately, but the feeling is incredible."*

*Jenny agreed: "For the first couple of weeks I was very satisfied emotionally. It was something I had really wanted for a long time. I really felt like this was the ultimate fulfillment."*

The vast majority of women give birth expecting the first few years of motherhood to be nonstop joy. They anticipate being totally fulfilled and happy with their lives, their child, their marriage. They assume everything will work out with relative simplicity. Media images have done a great deal to perpetuate this illusion. Magazine articles give the impression that it is easy to be a working mother. Television babies are never seen or heard except to be cuddled and shown off to friends. Certainly there are some exceptions—most of us familiar with "I Love Lucy" can still remember Lucy Ricardo asleep, bent over Little Ricky's crib after a rough night with the newborn, but those more realistic moments are few and far between on television.

Childbirth classes prepare women for giving birth. Parenting classes are concerned with the needs of the baby. When a new mother has a question about infant care or child development, there are hundreds of books in which she can find the needed information. Yet there is precious little material for the new mother on what is happening to *her*

GARLAND COUNTY
COMMUNITY COLLEGE
LIBRARY
Hot Springs, AR 71901

10/18/85

85-3/2

12.95 direct

body and what she may find herself feeling after she gives birth. Popular myths dictate that a woman's own motherly instincts will tell her everything she needs to know. She is, therefore, completely unprepared for so many new emotions and needs. She is shocked the first time she feels anger at her child or feels motherhood isn't the ultimate experience she expected it would be. She may feel inadequate when the nipple she attached pulls off the bottle, covering the baby with formula, or when her breasts hurt so badly from nursing that she dreads the next feeding. She is also unprepared for the lack of sexual desire she may feel, at a time when she had expected to be at her most emotional. New perceptions of herself, her husband, her marriage, and her life will begin to become apparent, and even upsetting, to her.

The first year of motherhood is a time of change, growth, and adjustment for virtually every new mother. The immense changes that a child will make in her life can be a complete surprise to her. There is no responsibility greater than caring for a tiny, totally dependent person. And that is what motherhood is really all about.

The purpose of this book, therefore, is to tell mothers what *they* may encounter during the first year. Whatever insecurities, fears, anger, and resentment they are experiencing have been felt before by many, many other mothers. They are normal and natural. To demonstrate the universality of the problem, many mothers from different socioeconomic, religious, and ethnic backgrounds have graciously told their stories and offered helpful hints for women in similar situations.

Monica described the changes that occurred in her marital relationship and her own unsatisfactory new perception of herself: "The first year could have killed our marriage. It didn't because of my husband's patience. I had no interest in sex. I resented that he didn't have to change his life to be a father, but I did to be a mother. I saw myself as having been reduced from a working woman to a mother. I was bored with the daily routine and felt my role was more limited and defined than it had ever been before. The baby was dependent on *me*, not us. I felt I was asking for permission to do things that I did without thinking before. I felt inferior and unhappy. Around the baby's first birthday things started looking up, and I realize now how strong our relationship must be for us to have survived that first year."

Laura added her own perspective: "I think the problem is that so much happens in such a short time. You have the baby, you become exhausted from never sleeping, you have to learn a whole new career, and at the same time you have to change your perception of yourself to include being a mother. You also start to worry about things that never mattered before. You're still adjusting to this little being, and you're out there writing wills, getting more life insurance and asking in-laws to be guardians, and you realize your whole outlook on your own life changed. It's all that responsibility."

The introduction of the newborn into the lives of its parents can be a tremendous jolt to their relationship and create strains and rifts they never thought possible. Instead of being idyllically happy, the couple may find themselves arguing more, feeling less secure in their marriage, and simply out of balance with each other.

As one family counselor commented, "If you have a really terrific marriage, don't screw it up by having a baby." In fact, studies have shown that roughly 80 percent of all couples said they were disturbed rather than pleased with the changed family situation after the arrival of the baby. Children tend to have a negative effect on a couple's sex life, social life, and time together. They often create financial problems. Masters and Johnson found that husbands who believed that marital infidelity for men was acceptable were often unfaithful for the first time during the first months after the birth of their first child.

"Our whole lifestyle changed. We couldn't run around with our friends at night, we stayed home much more. My husband went through a terrible crisis. He decided he was old before his time, that life was passing him by. It was a very difficult period of adjustment for both of us," said Karen.

Jenny felt that giving up her job to stay home with the baby had completely changed her concept of herself within the marriage relationship and had caused her husband and her to argue about money for the first time. "On an intellectual level I know I am pulling my own weight, but there is a nagging question of 'Am I really?' It has affected my needs. I need more support from him and more supportive relationships outside the home. I feel that every time I spend five dollars it's something we have to discuss and it will probably lead to an argument. I see patterns of arguing suddenly developing in our relationship that are frightening."

Sometimes the changing perceptions are good ones. Brooke found that, while she had some difficulty learning the new role of mother and becoming secure with it, she had a much higher appraisal of herself as a result. She explained: "I see myself as being much more capable of doing things than I used to. I feel very responsible now that I have proven I can take care of somebody else."

The changes that occur with the birth of a baby are so powerful that they do not go away but must be dealt with for months or even years. Medical journals and popular books tend to refer to the post partum as only the first three months after the baby is born, a fourth trimester of the pregnancy so to speak. The impression is that after the six-week checkup the process has ended and life begins to return to normal. However, only physical healing from the actual delivery has occurred by the sixth or eighth week. It may take up to three months just to achieve total physical healing. The post partum does not really end when the baby is three months old. Menstruating again doesn't mean the post partum is over; neither does the healing of the episiotomy stitches or the fact that the uterus has returned to normal. It may take the body a full year to regain some semblance of normalcy.

Eighty-five percent of the women interviewed said their sex drives did not return for at least ten months. Ninety percent of the nursing mothers and a few non-nursing mothers had pain with sexual intercourse for at least six months after the birth. Fatigue was described by most of the women as being a serious problem for nearly a year. The feelings of being trapped or bored, or feeling like a stereotype lasted nearly a year in most cases. Almost eighty percent experienced some degree of post partum depression which often didn't begin until the child was five or six months old and then engulfed the mother for weeks or months.

Single mothers had additional problems, including greater financial worries, the lack of a partner with whom to share the child's achievements and problems, and the lack of social life.

Almost all new mothers find that parenthood is not what they expected, their adjustment frequently takes a full year. This belies the illusion created by medical thinking that the post partum miraculously ends when the child is three months old.

"During the first year after the child is born you grow up," said Erica. "You learn for the first time to control and organize, but that takes almost a full year. You begin then to feel like an adult and a parent, and you realize that sometime during the fogginess and confusion you matured.

"I remember one day just before my son's first birthday a mouse ran into the kitchen. My son was in the playpen, and our cat was chasing the mouse around the room. My first instinct was to stand on the table and scream, but I said to myself, 'I can't do that. I am alone with the baby, I have to handle this.' And I did. I think it was then that I realized what motherhood was and what my life was going to be. Neither is what I expected."

Erica echoed the words of ninety percent of the mothers when she explained that the first months of motherhood were "as if you blacked out. Weeks and weeks went by and I was unaware of anything, even the passage of time. I just zeroed in on the baby's face, and that was my whole world. It changed my perspective, and it took almost a year to get back to normal. It takes that long to realize what has happened and that you must do something about it."

Having a baby is both a wonderful and a less-than-wonderful experience. There is probably nothing greater than watching your children grow as you love and nurture them. However, the responsibilities and demands of parenthood present a challenge that must be faced with understanding, patience, and a sense of humor. In this book you will read comments from many women who have offered to share their experiences. We also asked experts in family counseling, sex therapy, pediatrics, and corrective therapy for their thoughts and recommendations. You will find suggestions for coping with the large variety of problems and everyday questions that will arise as well as exercises for getting the figure back in shape after the delivery.

Nothing is sugar-coated or treated in an offhand manner in the chapters that follow. While the tale may sometimes seem a bit negative, it is told with love.

# CHAPTER TWO
# Countdown and Delivery

The post partum does not begin until after childbirth, but no book on a woman's feelings after the birth of her child would be complete without some discussion of the last few weeks of pregnancy and the labor and delivery. Many of the emotions, anxieties, self-doubts, and apprehensions a woman feels during these days of "Countdown and Delivery" are carried over into the post partum period and influence her recovery, so they must be described and understood before one can delve into the post partum.

By the ninth month of pregnancy a woman usually has experienced her first major mixed emotions regarding the birth and the child. On the one hand, she is eager to complete the pregnancy, which by this time feels as if it has lasted most of her adult life, and on the other she is acutely aware that she must give birth to an infant for that to happen. Giving birth, as everyone knows, can mean pain. It also means motherhood and a whole new set of crises for a woman to face.

How she copes with the discomforts of the last days of pregnancy, with the delivery, and with her first moments of motherhood can have an enormous influence on how she perceives herself during the post partum year and how quickly she accepts her new role and her relationship with the child.

As the end of pregnancy approaches the body balloons out, sometimes beyond the reach of off-the-rack maternity clothes. The baby's frequent kicking may deprive the woman of sleep, she may have frequent backaches from the position of the baby or the added weight, and she may feel like an automatic urinating machine.

Many women can't stand to look at themselves in the mirror by the last week of pregnancy. A woman's skin may be blotchy, and fluid increases may have given her face a spread appearance, broadening her nose or causing her lips to swell. Little vein spiders may have popped out on her nose and cheeks. Her contact lenses may be uncomfortable because of fluid changes in her eyes. She may feel like an unwed mother when out of the home because she can no longer wear her rings. Chemical changes in her body cause her skin to turn black under gold, or the rings may no longer fit because of added weight.

Many doctors recommend against sexual intercourse during the last few weeks of pregnancy. Add that to the unattractive looks a woman may have suddenly acquired, and it is no wonder the last weeks of pregnancy can put added stress on her emotional state and the couple's relationship.

The countdown period of the ninth month often, then, is not the blissful, exciting time of expectation most women imagine it will be. It can more closely be likened to a rocket-launching countdown. The pregnancy has reached the start of the final stage, but has been put in a holding pattern. It's five minutes and holding before liftoff, but since every case is individual the holding period may last a few days or a few weeks.

This holding stage can be very unpredicable. Practically everything the woman has read about the last few days, labor, and delivery *will not* happen. The more rigidly she expects to duplicate what she has read, the more likely she is to be disappointed with the birthing experience and her own performance. In fact, "unpredictable" is the code message of the entire delivery process and the days surrounding it.

# Sexuality

Even when the doctor does not recommend abstinence, sex may stop for many couples because the man avoids it. A surprisingly large number of husbands refuse to make love with their wives during the last weeks of pregnancy because they genuinely fear doing harm to the baby. Other men may refuse to have sexual relations of any sort because they feel they are imposing on the women in their delicate conditions. Such avoidance does not help the women's self-images as sexual beings, preceptions which are shaky enough by the last weeks of pregnancy.

Even when the husband is eager for lovemaking and continues to see his wife as a sexual being, it is perfectly normal for her to be unable to see herself that way. The physical effects of her pregnancy tend to reinforce any insecurity she may have previously felt about her looks. Many women exaggerate their fatness or unattractiveness in their minds because of self-images leftover from adolescence. If a woman always thought of herself as fat, she now sees herself as obese.

"During the entire third trimester of my pregnancy I had a very poor self-image," Nina explained. "I was very frustrated. I often found myself just looking in the mirror and crying. I thought I looked like a baby elephant, and I hated it."

To compound the problem of feeling unattractive and sexless, most women found they had a false, Madison Avenue image of what they would look like in their maternity clothes.

"Why is it everyone else always looks so cute?" asked Myra. "I saw clothes that looked great in magazines and on other women, but I never liked the way I looked through three pregnancies. I blamed it on the clothes, but deep down I guess I just didn't like the way my body looked."

In order to maintain their sense of sexuality during the last weeks of pregnancy, women must make more of an effort to be feminine and look their best. Remembering to wear make-up and buying a new outfit are ways of not only looking good, but making oneself feel good, a worthwhile effort.

# Fear of Pain

While approximately 4 percent of all women—usually women who already have many children—have totally painless childbirths (according to Aidan Macfarlane in *The Psychology of Childbirth*), every woman should be prepared for some pain. Certainly all first-time mothers can expect the delivery process to be painful and probably exhausting. It is called labor because of the work involved, and the delivering mother does work!

Of course, the word has been out for thousands of years. All women know labor and delivery can, and probably will, be very painful. In fact, womankind seems to have found a certain virtue in the pain, like a badge of courage or a mark of female martyrdom. There are few women who don't relish talking about all the pain they went through, and most have no qualms about passing on their experiences in vivid detail to anyone willing to listen. It is no more unusual to hear grandmothers recalling details of labors fifty years ago than it is to hear new mothers comparing notes. The experience is a life highlight that never loses its fascination.

For that reason, females are aware of the agonies of childbirth from a very young age. It is not surprising, then, that fear of the pain of labor and delivery and worry about how they will handle it are probably the most common anxieties faced by women approaching the birth of a child.

Even the history books remind us of the pain of childbirth and women's anticipation of that pain. It has been reported that in 1847, one of the first women in England to receive chloroform during childbirth was so thrilled with having the pain alleviated that she named her newborn daughter "Anaesthesia."*

One of the reasons for the popularity today of prepared-childbirth training, like Lamaze, seems to be this fear of pain. Childbirth classes teach that the pain is controllable—good pain, not something to be feared. Psychologically speaking, many women want that to be true. They want to believe the pain can easily be bypassed.

Ruth explained her deep-seated fears: "I was very anxious about the birth and about the pain. I took Lamaze training out of fear, because I felt it would reduce the pain. I was confused and frightened. I didn't

---

*Elizabeth Longford, *Queen Victoria, Born to Succeed* (Perennial Library, Harper and Row, 1964), p. 234.

want to feel the pain, but I was afraid of a spinal, and I didn't want to miss the birth. My doctor recommended the epidural* because of my fear, but I was so involved with my anxiety I couldn't digest what he was saying to me."

In fact, labor and delivery probably are more painful today than they were in generations past. Babies are bigger today, and bigger babies are more difficult to deliver. Babies are larger because:

1. Women today eat better, higher-protein diets.
2. The usually allowable 20 to 30 pounds weight gain during pregnancy seems to be better for the babies than the zero-weight-gain regimens of the last generation.
3. Fewer pregnant women smoke.

Prepared-childbirth courses provide women anticipating pain with a mythical panacea. They inadvertently teach them that if they are real women, they will conquer the pain and have control. Therefore, prepared childbirth has become almost a "must"—a real woman *must* do Lamaze and *must* prove her power over the pain.

"I believed Lamaze would make the delivery painless," said Ruth.

In *A Lamaze Guide: Preparation for Childbirth* by Donna and Rodger Ewy, the book recommended by most Lamaze instructors as a supplement to the classes, it clearly states: "Lamaze is not childbirth without pain" (page 33). The Lamaze method is meant to be an emotional, physical, and psychological preparation for childbirth. It is not a magical way to give birth both without anesthetics and without pain.

---

Epidural: A drug of the Caine family is given in a single dose or continuously through a catheter inserted into the peridural space in the lumbar region of the back. The woman is awake, but is numb from the waist down.

# How Will I Handle the Delivery?

Many women worry during the last weeks of pregnancy about how they will handle the actual labor and delivery and after the delivery worry still about whether they did well.

There seems to be an increasingly idealized insistence, perhaps fueled by the return to prepared forms of childbirth, that delivery should be perfect, not only in terms of the physical health of the mother and baby, but as an emotional experience for the parent.

There are also other indirect pressures that can make women feel they will somehow fail, or at least cheat themselves, if they don't have drug-free delivery.

Thus, women often wonder and worry in advance how well they will do during labor and delivery, as if they were part of a huge contest to have the most perfect delivery.

Each pregnancy, labor, and delivery is unique. Women are not in competition with each other to prove they are "earth mothers" with Phi Beta Kappa keys in childbearing. The doctor and delivery room nurses do not grade each mother on her performance, and the baby certainly doesn't know the difference.

Yet many women find they worry during the last weeks of pregnancy about how they will do and how much control they will have over the situation. They worry about embarrassing themselves with "less than womanly" behavior. And they worry about whether their delivery will reach a mythical level of perfection and whether they will achieve the overwhelming emotional experience they are anticipating.

"When my son was born, I really felt that I had failed, because I messed up the breathing exercise on two contractions. For weeks after the delivery I kept thinking about the fact that I wasn't able to hold my concentration through the whole labor and delivery. I thought that being able to do the Lamaze perfectly was normal and that I just wasn't handling it well," Erica admitted. "I kept thinking about the delivery over and over for at least two months. It really bothered me that I was imperfect."

In spite of the normalcy of reacting to the pain, many women expect that with the breathing exercises that should not happen. It is not unusual for a woman to admit that she believes she failed as a woman because she couldn't deliver without screaming.

It is not a failure to succumb to the pain. Since each labor and delivery is different and some are more painful than others, no woman should feel like a failure if she screamed and her friend didn't, or if she broke concentration and could not get it back. To quote again from the Ewy's book on Lamaze birth: "the aim of the training is not to make childbirth painless, but to make it a controllable, positive experience" (page 33).

# Hospital Registration

In many communities mothers-to-be avoid the problem of trying to register at the hospital while in the last minutes of labor by doing all the preliminary paperwork through the obstetrician's office. The nurses at the office will probably routinely give the expectant mother the forms she will need and will send them ahead to the hospital a few weeks before her due date. Thus, when she and the baby's father arrive at the hospital on delivery day they will only have to handle the final few forms needed for actual admission.

Women who have kept their own names after marriage would be well-advised to concede to the establishment and fill out all maternity-related hospital paperwork as Mrs. (husband's name). Although it may seem old-fashioned, the use of a married name is well worth it in paperwork saved later on. In some states if a child's mother and father are listed with different names at birth, the child is assumed to be illegitimate and will automatically be given the mother's name by the bureaucrat preparing the birth certificate. Straightening out records, which involves a lot of aggravation, is work new parents do not need. All women who use their own names should investigate state policy or simply play it safe and register in the hospital using the conventional married name combination.

# Labor Begins: The Trip to the Hospital

It has been shown on television many times—the hysterical trip to the hospital with Junior only moments from birth (or so we think).

Books and Lamaze instructors make it seem so easy. The pains will begin. There will be regular contractions, first about fifteen minutes apart, then gradually becoming six or seven minutes apart—at which time the couple, who have been coolly doing the Lamaze breathing and timing each contraction, will finally call the doctor.

From there it is an easy trip, which the couple has practiced (or carefully mapped out), to the hospital. Suitcase and Lamaze goody bag in hand, they leave for the hospital arm in arm, never missing a beat of the breathing exercises.

"I was having some pain," Laura described, "but it was two weeks before my due date, and the pains felt more like cramps than I imagined contractions would feel. At 8:00 P.M. we went to our Lamaze class. The instructor told my husband she thought it was labor, but I still didn't know what was going on.

"We went home, and he went to sleep. I started having terrible diarrhea and throwing up. At first I thought it was a virus or something, but when the pains became five to seven minutes apart consistently, I knew it was labor. We called the doctor, who told us to go to the hospital. Of course it was two weeks early, so I had nothing packed.

"There we were, running around trying to get a bag together and dress. My husband told me later he did three turns of the upstairs holding one of his socks. All I remember is that I kept yelling not to forget the lollipops.

"By the time we got to the hospital the contractions were very close together. We parked on the lot. Neither of us realized this was serious business and we should have parked by the emergency room entrance. We walked to the door. Every few steps I'd have a contraction, stop and do my Lamaze breathing. Finally I said 'Couldn't you have parked any closer?' The emergency room nurses saw that the contractions were so close together and whisked me upstairs in minutes."

Nina's trip to the hospital for the delivery of her second child was quite eventful. "Just as we were about to leave for the hospital, my son came flying around the corner of the living room, fell and hit his head on the coffee table. We all went to the emergency room together. I was in one examining-room cubicle, and my son was in the next. My husband had to keep going back and forth. It certainly took my mind off the labor."

Monica recalls that her labor went very quickly. She had gone from six minutes apart when she called the doctor to three minutes apart before they could get out of the house. "I was in such pain I knelt down on the floor and screamed, 'I'm going to have the baby right here.' My husband said, 'Oh no you're not' and somehow forced me to leave the house. Of course we raced to the hospital."

It seems reasonable to expect labor to follow the course depicted in books. That is, the length will be between eight and twelve hours for first-timers and between four and nine hours for repeat performers. In addition, the books say, women can expect each contraction to start slowly, increase in intensity, reach a crest and then subside. Each contraction will last about a minute, give or take thirty seconds. In reality, this may tell a woman nothing about what will happen during *her* labor.

"My contractions were not the way they described them in Lamaze," added Brooke. "They didn't start out low and then peak. They were just there. I couldn't get on top of them, so the breathing exercises didn't work."

It is important to remember that the length of the labor averages ten to twelve hours for the first baby. Therefore, except in rare cases there is ample time to get to the hospital. Most women expecting their first baby call the doctor too early and, as a result, end up spending a longer period than necessary in the confinement of the hospital labor room. Conversely, women expecting their second tend to wait too long, because they remember the first experience. Thus, with the second child there can be a classic race to the hospital with only minutes to spare.

Sometimes a woman experiences what she thinks is a labor of forty to sixty hours. Such labors are rare. What this woman is probably having is a long "warm up." She is having pains similar to contractions but is not in labor because her cervix is not dilating. Often this cannot be detected by the doctor during the middle-of-the-night phone call, because the woman has asked her mate to make the call. Many boring hours spent in the hospital could have been spent at home if women had spoken to the doctor directly. With the appropriate questions to the patient herself, most doctors can detect "warm up" time.

Donna, a Lamaze instructor herself, had pains resembling contractions for forty-nine hours. Only the last few were real labor. She went to see the doctor twice during the long wait and was able to spend most of her time at home, rather than confined in a hospital labor room.

"I started labor Tuesday night about nine, and my daughter was born Thursday night after ten," Donna explained. "I saw the doctor at his office Wednesday morning and Thursday afternoon. I finally went into the hospital about seven Thursday evening, and they gave me some pitocin.* Up till then my contractions had been regular and I was having strong ones, but they would space out. They'd be five minutes apart and then go back to fifteen minutes apart an hour later. The pitocin did the trick. The hospital staff was surprised at how fast I dilated after the pitocin. Of course, by the time the baby was born I was exhausted, very hungry and a little depressed from all the hours of waiting."

Jenny told us, "Between Lamaze and my mother's experiences, I had acquired a very optimistic view of labor and delivery. I assumed my water would break and I'd have a few hours of labor and then deliver. In reality I had a twenty-four-hour labor, and it was very rough.

"I kept telling my husband to forget the natural childbirth,—'If you love me, get me something for the pain.'—Then they'd offer me something and I'd refuse. Then I'd ask again. Finally they gave me twenty-five milligrams of Demerol, but I don't think it ever worked—at least it didn't feel as if the pain was ever reduced. I finally told my husband to go sit down and leave me alone. I was miserable. It was not

---

*Pitocin is the primary drug used to induce labor or to make the uterine contractions stronger or more effective during labor. It is also injected either intravenously or intramuscularly after delivery to make the uterus contract more rapidly to prevent bleeding.

at all what I had expected. I remember the Lamaze instructor saying to make sure you are focused really well so you won't be distracted by the untrained, screaming woman in the next room. I was trained and screaming away."

In fact, labor very frequently is not what the books and trainers lead women to believe. Even with the breathing and relaxation exercises taught in Lamaze and other training classes, the pain may make it difficult, if not impossible, to be as perfect as the woman may have hoped.

Even in the prepared-childbirth classes and books, the use of painkillers is discussed and suggested as an option if the pain becomes too intense during delivery. In fact, recent studies have shown that painkillers taken in moderation may be good for the baby as well as for easing the mother's situation. There is considerable evidence that the reduction of pain during the delivery process is good for the baby, because reducing pain in the mother may increase the oxygen supply to the baby.

Normal behavior for the delivering mother, even when Lamaze breathing is going well, may include various reactions to pain such as grimacing, grinding of teeth, tears, crying out, swearing, screaming, and demanding painkillers.

# I Felt Totally Dehumanized

It often comes as an unpleasant surprise to the laboring mother that, instead of being treated as a princess, she is subjected to a dehumanizing experience in which she is treated like any other hospital patient.

Instead of being fussed over, she enters the hospital labor room to find herself being examined and touched by everyone except the janitor. She had better forget modesty or any idea she had about this being a very private experience for herself and her husband.

Many women find they have barely undressed when a nurse is positioning them for an enema. After several dashes to and from the bathroom (which, unfortunately may not adjoin the labor room), a woman returns to her bed to find a nurse, and probably a hospital resident doctor. The doctor conducts a quick internal examination, after which the nurse shaves the area around the vagina.

If the labor is a long one, a woman may find herself being examined many more times by a variety of residents, her own doctor, and/or one or more of her doctor's partners.

If she has not had an enema, she may find she loses control during severe contractions and urinates or defecates on the bed, right in front of her husband and whatever hospital personnel are in the area. She may also find herself strapped to a fetal monitor, which means she cannot move. The contractions are painful, her back may begin to hurt, but she cannot move without a nurse's permission because in moving she may interrupt the signal of the monitor. Not only can't she move, but she is slowly becoming hypnotized by the beeps and lines— after all, her child's life is in those messages, and she dares not look away.

"They put me on the fetal monitor and told me they were sure from the signal that the cord was wrapped around the baby's neck," remembered Brooke. "I got nervous and started to hyperventilate, but I couldn't move. I could only move when they rotated me from side to side. They put oxygen in my nose because of the hyperventilating and continued to rotate me to decide whether the cord was tightening up on her neck. Then they gave me something to speed up the delivery, wheeled me into the delivery room, and three pushes later she was out. It was very strange. I was not in control at all."

Ruth recalled, "The most dehumanizing part of my second delivery was when the doctors examined me. They always talked as if I wasn't there. They mumbled things to the nurses or my husband and spoke of me in the third person. They kept examining me and mumbling things from the foot of the bed. They never spoke directly to me, so I couldn't digest what they were saying.

"I remember I asked for an epidural because I was in such pain, and all I heard was 'No.' My husband told me later that the doctor saw that I was going so quickly that I would deliver before the epidural could take effect, but he never said that to me. I was panicking, because I couldn't understand why they were withholding the epidural from me."

Laura said, "I was in the labor room with contractions very close together. The resident walked in, stood next to the bed and said to the nurse, as if I weren't even there, 'Tell her to start pushing.' Why couldn't he have said that directly to me?"

# The Power Play

Another reaction during labor that a woman does not expect, but that may occur, is somewhat akin to a power play with her husband. Since the father's role in the labor and delivery has become an active one with the return to "natural" forms of childbirth, most women expect the experience to be a joint one. They look forward to the anticipated moment of maximum closeness between them.

Instead, she may discover during labor that the last thing she wants is her husband hanging around. It may be just a need to control the situation herself, or, just as women have for generations, she may want to scream out her anger at this man "who caused her to go through such pain."

"I didn't want Tommy to touch me," said Faith. "I wanted to curse him. If he had offered any advice about my breathing, I would have screamed at him. It was my pain and my experience."

"I didn't realize it at the time because I had a long labor and I needed my husband to listen to the doctors and nurses for me because I was too out of it to really analyze everything," commented Geraldine. "But later, when I wrote the report for my Lamaze instructor, I realized that in nine pages I hadn't mentioned him once. It was my experience, and I had used him as sort of go-fer. When I realized it, I felt very self-centered."

Jenny said, "I told Brad to go sit down and leave me alone. It was my show. He was very supportive, but in terms of what was actually happening, I wanted to do it alone."

The man's role does become problematic for some women (and as a result for the doctor trying to assist with the delivery). Today men have been trained to be part of the delivery, but when it comes down to the wire, it is the woman's body that is the key and she must be able to do what is right for her body. Take-charge men often attempt to control the labor and delivery processes, leaving the woman torn between doing what she thinks he wants and expects and what her

College of the Ouachitas

body is telling her it needs. It is important that the husband be reminded he is a coach, not a manager. His role is to be supportive of her, not to advise her. She and the doctor must do what is right for her body.

# When Lamaze Works

The study done for this book was certainly not meant to be an examination of the Lamaze method of childbirth. Although it did indicate that about one-third of the women surveyed did not find that their labors and deliveries benefited from the Lamaze training, it also showed that an equal number thought Lamaze was excellent.

"It took me a good half hour to calm down and begin to concentrate on what I learned in Lamaze," explained Ina. "But I think it works extremely well if you really do exactly what the instructor taught you. And having my husband there the whole time definitely brought us closer together."

Jackie reported, "My labor was not what I had expected. First, it was very long...seventeen hours. Second, my daughter was in a posterior position, and they tried to turn her several times during the contractions. It was very painful. The Lamaze didn't deaden the pain any, but it did help me keep my mind off it. I knew what to do, and the relaxation breath calmed me down."

"I was in labor for seventeen and one-half hours," Valerie explained. "It was difficult because the baby was turned the wrong way and the doctor kept trying to turn her on each contraction. I thought the Lamaze breathing worked very well. I felt it was all relatively easy."

There is absolutely no way to predict what kind of labor a woman will have. Each case is unique. Therefore, each woman will have a different experience with whatever method she uses, be it Lamaze, epidural, or Caesarean.

Yet it is perfectly natural and normal for a woman to be anxious, not only about the labor, but about how well she will do in comparison to others. As Donna, the Lamaze instructor, put it, "I didn't want to make a fool of myself."

However, there really is no such thing as failing or seeming foolish. A woman who cannot manage the pain of labor is certainly no sillier that a man who refuses to participate in the delivery process because of his own anxieties. Each experience is as human and individual as the people involved. Some women experience very intense pain, some a bit less. You are delivering a baby, not taking a femininity test. No one fails. Everyone passes with an A, no matter what happens in the labor and delivery room.

# In the Delivery Room

## What Can Happen During Delivery

As delivery approaches, the woman—or more correctly today, the couple—anticipates a classic delivery, with father in the room. She will push, push, push, and the head will pop out. They will view it in a strategically placed mirror and cry with joy as the newborn is slipped out of the birth canal and placed on the mother's stomach. The cord will be cut, and they will hold their child lovingly as the doctor cleans away the placenta, stitches up the mother, et cetera.

That is probably true in one-third to one-half of all births. The delivery process may not be that straightforward, however, since many things can happen which will alter the picture.

Variations may occur because of a medical problem. A forceps (either suction or metal) may be needed to deliver a baby with a large head. If the cord is wrapped around the child's neck a faster delivery may be induced or a Caesarean performed. Suspicion that the oxygen supply to the baby has been reduced may require the mother to wear an oxygen mask and necessitate faster delivery. Occasionally the baby arrives before the woman can be fully prepped by the nurses. One woman told the story of her sister's very fast delivery: she stood up in the labor room, and the baby dropped out. Fortunately the doctor was able to catch it.

In a very small number of cases, women have experienced virtually no labor pains at all. Connie reported not experiencing any pain with any of her four children. "I just kind of knew it was time," she said. "I'd call the doctor and say, 'I think the baby is coming,' have a friend drive me to the hospital and deliver within a short time. There would be a little discomfort with the last minutes of delivery itself, but nothing like what other people talk about."

It is possible to have a delivery like Connie's or to have the classic, predictable labor and delivery depicted in the media, but no one should go into the experience so convinced that she will have the ideal situation that she cannot adapt should there be a surprise.

Anything goes. The range of what may be considered completely normal is quite wide when one speaks of delivery. Thus, a woman who goes into the hospital with high expectations of what will happen— the classic picture from books and the movies—may be in for a surprise and even an emotional letdown when her delivery appears to be "abnormal."

# The Post Partum Begins

Officially, the post partum begins when the baby enters the world. As the head "crowns"(begins to push through the vaginal opening), excitement starts to build, then suddenly the baby is out and it becomes another person to be dealt with in the family unit.

If all is going without complications, the doctor will probably place the baby on the mother's stomach, while the nurse will quickly suction any fluid out of its mouth and the cord will be clamped. The mother will probably get to hold the child before the nurse takes it away to clean it.

After a few minutes for cleaning, the baby is usually given to the father, and then back to the mother. The degree of bonding with the parents that takes place varies widely. Some doctors or hospitals allow the baby to stay only a few minutes, preferring the couple to be alone to share this time of intimacy. Other facilities allow the baby to stay with the parents for an hour or more for bonding as a family.

Bonding aside for the moment, a surprisingly large number of women react immediately with disappointment at this crucial time, a feeling they try to rationalize for weeks afterward.

Donna was surprised at her own reactions, "I expected elation and the desire to ooh and ah over the baby. Instead, I had such mixed feelings. I was happy to have her, but I was exhausted and happy it was over, too. It was confusing."

Estelle remembers: "I was lying there laughing like crazy because the baby was two pounds larger than the doctor expected."

"My first reaction was pleasure at having the delivery that I had dreaded for so long over with. I was also terribly embarrassed, because I hadn't had an enema and I delivered a small BM just before the head crowned," said Ruth. "Then I felt like a queen because I had given birth to such a perfect being."

A brief period of feeling let down is not at all unusual after delivery. The anticipation has been so high, so much was expected of the experience, yet the woman is tired, emotionally drained, and physically worn out. In terms of muscle usage, labor is extremely exhausting. Experiencing a brief feeling of "Is that all there is?" can be perfectly normal.

# The Caesarean Mother

Having a Caesarean, or C-section, can be enormously traumatic for some women. They have been anticipating that moment of delivery, perhaps idealistically, and it is abruptly taken away.

Since an increasing number of C-sections are being performed annually, it has become a real possibility that a woman may take Lamaze training, begin labor normally and, after many hours of carefully doing the exercises, suddenly find herself being rushed into the delivery room or operating room, given an epidural or general anesthesia and delivering without participating.

Many women feel defeminized by the experience. They feel cheated or less womanly because they could not deliver vaginally. This may color their reactions to the child and be a cause of post partum depression in the weeks after birth.

There can be many reasons a doctor recommends a C-section. He/she may see some problem in advance, such as an obvious pelvic disproportion or a baby in the breech position, or past surgery on the uterus. However, most C-sections are recommended in the hospital after many hours of labor have elapsed with some difficulty appearing, or in cases of clear risk to the mother or child (for example, should the placenta be too low or separate from the uterine wall, or should the cord prolapse, or should the baby go into distress from the stress of labor).

One reason for the apparent increase in Caesareans in recent years is the improvement in monitoring equipment which enables the physician to have a better idea when there are problems or risks involved.

Certainly there are elements of the medical/legal crisis which affect the growing number of C-sections done today. Doctors are admittedly afraid of malpractice suits should an infant be born with a defect that could have been prevented had a Caesarean been performed, so they tend to opt for the Caesarean if the monitoring devices indicate a level of fetal distress that gives them cause for concern. However, most doctors also believe that Caesareans have been one reason for the birth of better, healthier babies in many cases.

Mona's C-section was decided upon about three days before the delivery. "I had a history of ovarian cysts and surgeries. About three weeks before my due date the doctor found that the baby was in the wrong position, so he began watching the situation. The day after my due date he sent me for a x-ray. The baby had not turned. It would have been a risky delivery even for someone without my medical history, but the doctor gave me the option. I chose to have a C-section to be safe. Three days later she was delivered. I had an epidural because I wanted to be awake. They let me hold her in the delivery room right after she was born, and I was very excited."

Geraldine and Nancy had Caesareans after many hours of labor. Geraldine went through seventeen hours of labor. "I was in excruciating pain from back labor, and nothing was happening. After seventeen hours I had dilated only about three centimeters," she remembered. "The doctor sent me for a pelvimetry, a pelvic x-ray. It showed that I had a big baby and a small pelvic opening. Delivering her safely via the birth canal would have been risky. The doctor said I had two choices: continue the labor with some pitocin or other help in inducing dilation, or have a Caesarean. We chose the C-section without hesitation. It had been long enough. I had an epidural. My husband was in the delivery room with me, and he held the baby for several minutes while they sewed me up. It was a very happy and emotional experience for both of us. I don't regret choosing the C-section."

Nancy had a similar experience. She recalled, "With my second baby I went all the way through labor, about nine hours, and the doctor couldn't turn the baby. He was coming out face forward, a position that is not deliverable safely through the vagina. The doctor said I had to have a C-section. I knew it was a necessity, so it was fine. I have back problems, so I couldn't have an epidural. I was put under general anesthesia. I remember the feeling when I woke up and the anesthesiologist said, 'You have a nine-and-a-half-pound boy.' I was ecstatic."

Since these women believed there was a sound medical reason for their C-section, none experienced any recriminations or soul-searching afterward.

While having a Caesarean after months of anticipating a vaginal delivery can be a disappointment, it is certainly not a sign of some failing as a woman. Especially today, when women can have many births by Caesarean, not just one or two as previously believed (some women may have later babies by vaginal delivery even if the first is a Caesarean), the C-section mother is every bit as much a woman as her vaginally delivered counterpart. She may even be luckier: after all, she did not have an episiotomy, so her erogenous zones are still intact.

# Midwives and Home Deliveries

The midwife is once again gaining in popularity as a replacement for the obstetrician during the delivery. Some midwives even deliver in hospitals, and in many rural areas they still function as the primary care agent in deliveries.

A midwife working in a hospital is similar to a general or family practitioner delivering the baby. As long as there are no complications, midwives can do the job quite well, and in the hospital setting there is an obstetrician on call in case of emergency. Within the hospital, midwives conduct the delivery similar to the way an obstetrician would: They usually perform an episiotomy, they are assisted by the regular delivery-room nurses, and they have all the best sanitary conditions available for the new mother and child. Many women feel they receive a more personalized touch from the midwife than they might from a doctor and feel more comfortable with the less authoritative figure of the midwife during the delivery.

Home deliveries, whether with a midwife or a doctor (even an obstetrician), are considered by most medical authorities to be a dangerous return to the past. The lack of ideal sanitary conditions and emergency equipment should it be needed can be a great risk to the health of both the mother and the baby. It is unnecessary in this day and age to increase the risk of infections or take the chance that the baby will need medical care that will not be immediately available.

In recent years another choice, the alternative birthing center, has begun to appear in many parts of the country. Birthing centers are not hospitals. They are small facilities that maintain sanitary and medical practices, but have a homier warmth about them than hospitals and permit deliveries by either midwives or doctors. Anyone who does not feel comfortable with the idea of delivering in a hospital might want to seek out the nearest birthing center rather than to deliver at home. However, often one cannot predict when there may be a complication during delivery which birthing centers are not equipped to handle. The best situation is to be in a hospital with the latest equipment and a humanitarian attitude.

# The Baby Is a Person

There is no question that the majority of women respond to the new being whom they have created with feelings of joy, delight, and even ecstacy. However, a surprisingly large number of women, perhaps as many as one-quarter of all new mothers, are embarrassed that their immediate reactions aren't so enraptured.

Many find they have mixed feelings, or are disappointed by the shriveled human beings with red marks on their faces that are allegedly their progeny. One new mother remarked, "It was something of a letdown. You build up to this point for nine months, expecting the most wondrous experience of your life, and suddenly it's all over and it was painful and exhausting, not thrilling. Seeing the baby is almost an anticlimax."

Those women who do feel this letdown immediately after delivery often feel guilty—the first trace of mother's guilt, which may become a familiar companion over the next few decades. Others react more strongly. For them it is the start of a more severe post partum depression. But women who do not immediately exult in their children are not alone. Many, many mothers do not react with delirious joy upon first viewing their babies. Generally, after a nap and some food the letdown passes and happiness sets in.

In the majority of cases, the mother does react immediately as she may have expected. She laughs, cries and forgets all about the labor and delivery. As Jenny put it, "The pain was much more than I expected and I was miserable, but as soon as I saw the baby I forgot about the whole thing and was ready to do it again."

"They gave my daughter to me even before they cut the cord," remembered Vikki. "She was covered with all that gunk and she was still beautiful."

Whenever possible today, couples are given time to "bond" with the baby. They hold and play with the child before it is taken to the nursery. Some mothers even attempt to nurse on the delivery table or in the hallway outside the delivery room, if they are allowed to rest there with the child for any length of time. Even Caesarean couples often get to bond with the child if the woman did not have general anesthesia. In cases where there is some reason to be concerned about the health of either the child or the mother, however, bonding is not recommended and the baby is usually taken immediately to the nursery. Although today's popular childbirth training programs strongly urge bonding, the mothers surveyed who did not get the opportunity did not feel cheated, nor did they feel it interferred at all with their natural closeness to the child.

Studies have shown that bonding is more helpful to the parents than to the child. There is little evidence that immediate bonding has any effect on the newborn's adaptation to life or to its parents, but there is some proof that it helps the parents, especially the father, develop good feelings toward the child. Since the man's role in the delivery is peripheral, in spite of prepared-childbirth training, bonding makes him feel closer to the woman and the child. While the involvement of the father in the delivery process has added a new dimension to childbirth for many couples, bonding with the child shortly after birth seems to be of greater effect and can be offered even to fathers who were too squeamish to watch the actual delivery.

Bonding can be delightful or tiring. It is a lovely experience when it can be enjoyed. Missing the opportunity to bond is understandably disappointing to a couple who have been planning for it, but it does not portend some failing in the parents. How much the baby's behavior may be affected by being handled by its parents immediately after birth is still very much an open question, as is the effect bonding may have on the mother's emotional well-being.

An old wives' tale about the delivery process says that if a woman can remember her labor pains, she won't have another child. Of course, most women can remember and talk about the pain. They especially will talk about anything unusual that happened during the delivery, but they can have more children in spite of these memories.

The old wives were wrong. Remembering means nothing if it's not important. And most women find that, once they have that tiny person in their arms, the pains, the problems of pregnancy, labor and delivery just *don't matter*. The emotions of new motherhood and the marvelous ability of the baby to mesmerize its mother are what will really count.

CHAPTER THREE
# In the Hospital

For most new mothers, the first three to four days after delivery are spent in a hospital maternity unit (an average of eight days for Caesarean mothers). Unless they have "rooming in" (having the baby in the room with them all or most of the time), they see and hold their babies for less than an hour four or five times each day.

Some mothers find the amount of contact with the child sufficient, some crave more, others turn down encounters between midnight and six in the morning, opting instead for more rest. But for all of them, whether they are first-, second-, or fifth-time mothers, the time spent with the baby during the first few days is a unique learning experience.

Every child is a new and different experience for the mother. She must adapt and adjust emotionally and practically. In those first few days she begins to confront her concept of motherhood and her image of herself within the family unit. She also must begin to accept and understand the baby itself. It is an individual, with natural human needs and needs peculiar to its own personality. First-time mothers must become proficient at a completely new set of skills—breast- and/or bottle-feeding, dressing a baby, diapering, and so forth. Also, there are the leftover fatigue and emotions from the delivery and the hospital routine with which to deal. The vision of a trouble-free life of loving and cuddling for the parents and the baby belongs only to the television commercial in which it thrives. Reality is much more work.

# Physical Realities

During the first few days, the new mother can expect to feel a bit worn out physically from the effects of the labor and delivery. She may also have "afterpains," cramps which are caused by the uterus contracting to reduce blood loss and empty itself. Afterpains can occur for a few weeks but are most severe during the first two or three days after delivery. Most first-time mothers said they were unaware of the afterpains, which are more severe with subsequent deliveries.

Lochia, the bloody discharge that will continue for three or four weeks, will be at its heaviest during the first week. Episiotomy pain or discomfort varies from woman to woman. Some women described minor discomfort for a day or two, while others complained of more severe pain for days or weeks. The degree of episiotomy pain experienced is directly related to each individual's natural healing mechanism and the size of the cut and cannot be predicted or generalized.

Caesarean mothers will probably have some difficulty moving for the first forty-eight hours, but the nurses will undoubtedly insist that they get out of bed the first day. While this forced, painful movement may seem cruel, it is necessary to encourage circulation in the veins of the legs and pelvis to help avoid clotting. In addition to the pain of the surgery and the afterpains, a Caesarean mother may also have intense cramps from gas on the second to fourth days. The pain, which is similar to colic, is the natural result of the break in eating patterns which accompanies surgery.

Nursing mothers will begin to experience some breast tenderness and, by the third day in the hospital, may feel engorged and swollen or sore.

Other problems may include an infection in the bladder, a slight burning during urination if the woman is not drinking enough, or on the surface from the shave. She may experience some constipation because she is afraid to push for fear of tearing the stitches. Impacted feces (stool that is very hard because all the water has been drawn out of it) may occur in rare cases.

Many women find these minor pains incidental and do not let them interfere with their enjoyment of the baby or chatting with friends and family who come to visit. Some even described being so happy they were only vaguely aware that they were having some discomfort.

# Confronting Motherhood

Motherhood has two components: One is the emotional, the other the physical taking care of the child. Both are faced head-on by the new mother in those first few days in the alien environment of the hospital.

About one-third of all new mothers have a delayed reaction to the newborn. This may mean days, or even months, before they feel emotionally the way they had anticipated. An overwhelming outpouring of maternal love may not be an automatic response for many women.

This question of delayed "maternicity" is so common that many studies have been done to try to determine some pattern. New mothers have been studied to see if their age at the time of delivery is a factor, or their worries related to the baby, or whether bonding on the delivery table can make a difference, or whether difficulty in the delivery process had some effect, or whether their fear of disappointing the husband because of the baby's sex, or their own discomfort with handling one particular sex could be the cause. The results have been inconclusive.

Research in England had indicated that hormonal build-ups may be part of the cause, but adjustment to the idea of being a mother and having such an enormous responsibility thrust upon oneself probably has at least equal effect.

Whatever the root of the reaction, it is a self-feeding problem. If a woman finds she isn't instantly madly in love with the child, she can feel inadequate, selfish, unfit for motherhood, or simply disappointed in herself and the child. She is sure there is something wrong with her, because she had this terrible, insensitive reaction. This upsets her and makes it even more difficult for her to relax and enjoy the baby.

Some experts on family interaction believe that no parent loves a newborn immediately. They theorize that while most people feel a certain bond with the child, it cannot be called "love" for many weeks or even months. Love, they argue, is a response that must grow slowly within us. Again, this is just theory, as are all the other possible explanations for the frequency of delayed maternicity.

The crux of the issue is that a woman coming to terms with her newborn and her feelings about that child in the controlled environment of the hospital can easily find she does not experience an overwhelming rush of maternal love. If that happens, she has not failed the first test of motherhood. The hospital is a very protective place, an environment very different from home. Once the mother and child are home and mother is "flying solo" in terms of caring for and handling the child, she is much more likely to begin to develop deep feelings for the infant.

# I Don't Know What to Do

The second test of motherhood most women assign themselves is how well they handle the physical care of the baby.

Unless a woman has taken care of an infant at some time, she may suddenly realize that she has no idea what to do with the child who is handed to her by the nurse. What is she doing with a baby? She has never even held an infant before, let alone changed or fed one.

"I can remember being with a friend with a six-month-old during my pregnancy," laughed Laura. "I had never been with children at all. There was this baby spitting up on the floor. I thought, my child will never do that. Little did I know!

"When our son was born, I still knew nothing," she continued. "I think I imagined something idyllic in which the baby slept all day and I would watch adoringly. The first time he was with me and let out a little 'eh,' I panicked. I began to sweat and turn red. Thank goodness my husband had helped raise a cousin and knew about babies. I was so unprepared it was ridiculous."

Mona recalled, "I remember they brought me my daughter the morning after she was born and I was afraid to unwrap the blanket around her because I was sure I wouldn't be able to rewrap it."

"The first time they brought me the baby I was very nervous and afraid to be alone with her," Jackie mused. "I suddenly realized that I had never held a baby before and knew nothing about them."

In fact most mothers judged the level of nursing care they received in the hospital totally by the amount of help they felt they had received in relationship to baby handling and care. If the nurses had eased their insecurities and been extremely instructive they were considered good; any deviation from that made them seem inadequate.

# Feeding/Nursing

Most women assume that the baby will automatically nurse when put to the breast, or suck when given a bottle. This is not necessarily true. While sucking is one of the instinctive reflexes the baby has at birth, the infant does not always know exactly how to do it with maximum efficiency. Some babies are born with less developed sucking mechanisms, which can make their first attempts at eating challenging for both mother and child. In addition, even if the baby can suck without encouragement, it may not be able to swallow at the same rate it takes in the milk, thus causing gagging.

Other animals do not have large breasts with small nipples, their breasts are utilitarian and designed for feeding the infant. The evolution of the human breast has created an instrument that is not perfectly designed for its nursing task. The human nipple does not go in the baby's mouth deeply enough for the baby to suckle easily. The infant's noseway may become blocked, and mouth breathers fight the nipple because it is difficult for them to let go to breathe and then grab the nipple again. Thus, breast-feeding a human infant is not automatic, but a skill that must be learned by both the mother and the child.

"It was a good thing that I was so nervous that I insisted the nurse stay the first time I nursed," said Jackie. "As I was trying to feed the baby she started gagging. I had no idea what to do and panicked completely. The nurse grabbed her and suctioned out her mouth, and she was fine. Then I started crying, because if the nurse hadn't been there I don't know what I would have done."

Some hospitals have very well-organzied systems for teaching new mothers how to breast-feed more easily, while others leave it up to the individual nurses. If there is a large number of mothers and babies in the maternity wing, it is often difficult for the nurses to instruct each woman unless she specifically requests help. Several women complained that they were at a loss for the first few days and suggested that some uniform system of mother education be developed for hospitals, especially now that so many women are electing to breast-feed.

"They brought the baby in, handed her to me and walked out," said Faith. "They also left a syringe, cotton balls, a bottle of sugar water, and a rubber nipple shield on the nightstand. It didn't occur to me until weeks later that the syringe was to be used to suction out her mouth if she started to choke. Fortunately I hadn't needed it, but what if I had? The whole thing was left up to me. There I was alone with my baby and my breasts, and I was supposed to know what to do."

"I was having trouble getting her to nurse well," said Geraldine. "I'd put her to the breast and she'd make little effort to suck, so after twenty minutes or so I'd think 'Well, she has to eat something,' and give her the sugar water the nurse had left. Then the nurse would come in and berate me for not making a greater effort to nurse. On the third day there was a different nurse, who helped me a lot. After that it was fine."

Today it has become fashionable for women to try to nurse their newborns on the delivery table within minutes of birth. Many doctors feel this may not be advisable, because it may interfere with the baby's need to learn how to breathe on its own. Once it is clear that he/she is swallowing and breathing normally, nursing can be started safely. Contrary to popular opinion, nursing on the delivery table does not speed up the involution process of the uterus. That is faster and more efficiently controlled by the pitocin the doctor administers immediately after the placenta is delivered.

Nursing is not as easy and automatic to begin as it might appear. True, women all over the world, in even the most primitive cultures, nurse, but they usually have mothers and other elders to help them. Women in today's childbearing generation in America may very well need help from nurses or other trained personnel. In all probability their mothers did not nurse them. Probably, too, their mothers think they are crazy to nurse when formulas are so easy to obtain.

"I thought it was very funny," said Mona. "Both my mother, who had not nursed, and my mother-in-law, who nursed all six of her children, thought I was very peculiar because I wanted to nurse. Thank goodness my sister-in-law is a nurse. She gave me lots of help."

Not only may it be difficult to get the baby to suck, or even to show any strong interest in nursing, but the first physical effects the experience may have on the mother can begin to set in before she leaves the hospital. Sore nipples and engorged, sore breasts can be an unpleasant surprise for the new nursing mother. These effects will get worse before they get better over the next two weeks (see chapter 4).

# Hospital Routine

Whatever else can be said for them, hospitals are very routinized and organized places. The day starts very early, so that patients can be fed and readied before the doctors begin their rounds (usually around eight o'clock). Food is generally bland, and patients' temperatures are taken at regular intervals. The normal routines do not vary much even on the maternity floor.

The first thing any patient should do is try to learn something about hospital policies and become acquainted with the hospital and its paraphernalia. How does one call the nurses? How does the bed work? Learn what all the various buttons do.

"The room I was in had the communications system with the nurses' station built into the TV which hung over the bed," remembered Geraldine. "I never thought to ask. The baby was born on Friday night, and on Saturday night—really Sunday morning— about 4:00 A.M. suddenly the TV over my head lit up and a voice said, 'They're bringing your baby now.' Caesarean stitches and all, I came very close to leaping out of bed. What a shock! Next time I'll ask questions *before* I go to sleep."

Normally there are more nurses on the day shift than the night. On a maternity floor the nights are usually uneventful, so usually one registered nurse and an aide or two are enough. The day-shift head nurse is the senior nurse of all three shifts. Should there be any problem, the day head nurse is the one to speak to.

In addition, too few patients realize that their doctor is really their ombudsman, their spokesperson, with the nurses and hospital administration. If anything disturbs a patient, she should feel completely comfortable about telling her doctor when he/she comes for rounds the next day—or, if the problem is immediate, telling the obstetrical intern or resident or the house doctor, who will call your doctor.

A hospital is not a hotel or a spa, it is an institution for health care which is concerned primarily with the care of patients and medical practices. A maternity patient will be checked regularly, as will her baby. They will both be fed, and they'll be given clean sheets daily and whatever medical help may be required. This will be done as efficiently as possible, usually with a smile or a pleasant word. However, most hospitals today are understaffed, so individual special attention may not be possible unless there is a medical reason to warrant it.

# What to Expect from Nurses

Most women have had an excellent experience with maternity floor nurses, but since care given often reflects the number of patients on the floor, service varies. Obviously, if there are only two or three new mothers and babies in the maternity unit, care will be greater than if every room is full and two nurses and two aides are spread among thirty women (there are additional nurses and staff in the nursery who care only for the babies).

Many women go into the hospital believing that the nurses will automatically instruct them in every phase of child care from diapering to breast-feeding. Often this picture of the nurse who will spend long periods of time giving instructions and assistance to each mother is the result of things the women have been told in their prepared-childbirth classes. Unfortunately, no one told the floor nurses.

In a well-managed hospital, the floor nurses and nursery nurses will all be willing to help a patient, but often she must ask for the help. Nurses are not mind readers. A smiling, inquiring woman who is obviously a bit unsure of herself with the child will get a good response from the nursing staff if she asks for help. No mother should feel embarrassed to ask. Not knowing isn't a sign of incompetence, just of being new to the game. Generally, the babies are delivered to the mothers by aides or volunteers who are very sweet, but can offer no help. However, if a nurse is requested she will come to the room as soon as her duties permit.

It is wise not to begin asking questions of the nurses in the early morning when the pediatricians and obstetricians are making rounds, or while the beds are being made up, because that is when the nurses are the busiest. However, the baby feeding time and the pre-lunch period when there are few visitors, are excellent times to ask questions.

Ask what to do, ask for advice on handling, feeding, anything that is unclear. If breast-feeding is a problem, ask any nurse about giving you an oxytocin nasal spray. This nasal spray has no side effects and will help speed up the "letdown" reflex. It is an enormous help to many new mothers. The nurse can quickly phone the doctor's office and obtain permission to give the spray to women who are having difficulty with early nursing. One quick spray into each nostril a few minutes before nursing can make the milk flow easily and alleviate much of the pain from the baby's sucking. The spray probably won't be needed after the woman is fully lactating—a matter of only a few days—but it can be very helpful during those first few days. Women who have received the spray swear by it.

Ask questions, too, about the schedule the hospital uses for the babies in the nursery. Donna, a nurse and Lamaze instructor, once worked in the nursery of the hospital in which she later gave birth. She now cautions all her Lamaze students to beware. There is an excellent reason why babies have their most active periods between three and five in the morning when they first come home from the hospital, she confided. Since that is a very quiet, boring time, that is when the nurses and aides in the nursery play with the newborns and give them their baths.

Almost all hospitals offer classes on how to bathe the baby, how to diaper, and a variety of other subjects which the new mother should make the effort to attend.

# Residual Effects of the Delivery

Many women find that even if they are extremely happy with they baby and their first hours of motherhood, they still find themselves dragging for the first day or two after the birth.

Pain from the stitches and general fatigue seem to be the most frequently heard complaints. Such weariness or achiness is to be expected. Delivery is hard work under any circumstances. The longer it takes, the longer the recovery may be. A woman who was in labor from nine at night until she finally delivered at one the next afternoon should expect to be too tired to really enjoy her baby until she has had some sleep.

# Missing Pieces

A woman may find that the residual effects she has from the delivery are mental or emotional. This is particularly true if she can't remember everything that happened during the labor and delivery. Any gaps or "missing pieces" can cause great anxiety and self-doubts the next day.

Researchers have found that 70 percent of all women cannot remember their labor and delivery completely. Each woman found there were some events she simply could not recall. These time gaps are similar to retrograde amnesia. It is as if nature is providing the ability to forget some of the tiring or painful aspects of labor. However, many women who experience "missing pieces" quiz doctors and nurses at length to try to fill in the gaps. They become almost obsessed with trying to recall the lost moments, often adding things that didn't happen or some distortion to what did in their desperation to remember.

In the days after the birth they feel a residual disappointment because they can't remember the exact sound of the baby's first cry or the details of their time in the delivery room. Such women often find themselves daydreaming about the delivery in an effort to remember, or having recurring dreams about the delivery. These dreams provide something of a therapy, because they allow the woman to cope with the childbirth crisis and her disappointment at not experiencing everything exactly as she had imagined.

The attempt to search for the missing memories usually fades after a few days; however, for some women it does remain for many weeks, months, or even years.

# Highs and Lows

For most women the first few days post partum are marked by extreme highs and lows. One minute the new mother may be just thrilled to be reminded that she has parented such an absolutely perfect, beautiful child, and the next minute she can be struck by enormous doubts. "I did it!" can easily be transformed a few hours later into "What have I done?"

Pride when the child is praised can become an introspective "I'm not equipped to be the mother of this perfect child" minutes later.

A woman will probably never make a bigger adjustment both physically and emotionally, so such topsy-turvy reactions are perfectly normal. Not only is she an emotional mess—she is happy, yet awed by her new responsibilities, exhilarated, yet tired from the birth itself— but she is going through a hormonal change unrivaled by any other moment in her life. Her entire body is flip-flopping from pregnant to not pregnant, or from pregnant to nursing. Estrogen is down, prolactin is up and oxytocin is beginning to develop so she can lactate. Her body doesn't know whether it is coming or going. Why shouldn't she be hyperemotional and unpredictable?

"The second day after he was born I was rocky," Monica remembered. "It was as if my body were the ocean. I was rocking back and forth, and it was an uncomfortable feeling. I was on too much of a high and at the same time in a complete fog."

# The Baby Blues

Perhaps the most talked about aftereffect of childbirth is the infamous post partum "baby blues," the mild depression that seems to attack many women the second or third day after the baby is born. Researchers have concluded that anywhere from half to three-quarters of all new mothers have an attack of the "baby blues" within the first three days; a few more seem to have a delayed reaction within a week or so after the birth.

The causes of "baby blues" are many. There is the stress and fatigue inherent in childbirth. Hormonal changes are occurring very rapidly in the postnatal woman. The emotional strain, excitement, and perhaps letdown, of the delivery and immediate post partum add to the "blues," as do a woman's thoughts of the new responsibiltiies and questions about her adequacy as a mother. Together these ingredients can combine to cook up a short, but upsetting, period of depression.

Women who are experiencing "baby blues" may find that they cry suddenly, for no apparent reason or on the slightest provocation. They may feel restless, confused, or highly fatigued. If they do not have actual insomnia, they will probably have fitful, frequently interrupted sleep, and they will find it difficult to concentrate. The "baby blues" usually stays for only a day or two, but cases have been reported that lasted for up to ten days and this is not considered unusual.

"I remember with my second child I had a really terrible day the third day," Nina said. "My milk came in that day, and I felt miserable. I wanted to just crawl in a corner."

Dorian remembered, "I had a blue day with my second child while I was still in the hospital. I became very depressed because the whole thing was over. The thing I had looked forward to so much was over. Now I had a baby to contend with. I can remember calling up one of my friends and crying."

"The last night in the hospital I was literally hysterical," Vikki recounted. "Everything panicked me. The nurse hadn't shown up at our house on time and the store had delivered the wrong furniture for the baby, and I got hysterical. I was so upset my in-laws drove forty miles to the store to get the furniture situation straightened out that night."

Post partum "baby blues" can be a sign of a more severe depression that will increase in intensity as the months go by (see chapter 8), but for the vast majority of women it is merely a mild depression that seems to be a natural reaction to childbirth, at least in modern, industrialized Western countries.

# Rest

Perhaps the most universal complaint of new mothers is that they did not get sufficient rest while in the hospital. It does seem to be true that maternity floors of modern, American hospitals are not the best place to be if one needs one's sleep.

Even though babies are generally kept in a nursery that is somewhat removed from the mothers' rooms and enclosed for quiet and the protection of the infants, most women swear they were kept awake all night by the sounds of babies crying.

In fact, babies do travel up and down the halls en route to their mothers for feeding periodically during the night. Especially in recent years, when so many women are once again nursing, babies are brought to their mothers as they are ready between midnight and six in the morning. In addition, "rooming in" is quite popular today. If a baby that is rooming with its mother has a bad night, probably all the women in nearby rooms will hear it.

Most women interviewed recommended against the semiprivate room. They agreed that the extra cost for a private room was well worth it for a myriad of reasons.

Your roommate's baby may be brought in for feedings in the wee hours at a completely different time than your baby (they bring in babies as they wake up). Thus, while you may want to sleep, you may be awakened by her baby being brought in, crying, etc.

Many women mentioned that their roommates had insomnia and paced all night or watched television, keeping them awake, too. A few women had roommates with problems that necessitated nurses coming in and out with drugs, again awakening both the women, the ill one and the tired roommate. Personal habits such as smoking can become a major irritant. Doctors explain that no hospital patient should have to put up with a bad roommate situation. You can ask to be moved, and you should for your own rest and peace of mind.

Only one woman said she was able to get a lot of needed rest in the hospital—a woman who had a private room and did not nurse. She allowed the night staff to give the baby its middle-of-the-night bottle. All the other women said that, for one reason or another, by the time they arrived home they were utterly exhausted.

# Visitors

One of the reasons cited for lack of rest in the hospital was an overabundance of visitors.

"Most of my friends were nice," recalled Vikki. "They called first to see if I was awake enough for visitors or if there was anything I needed. But I never got any rest because of my in-laws' friends. Every time I thought I was having a breather, another of their friends would come in."

Some hospitals restrict the number of visitors who can be in a room at one time and have short visitors' hours which limit visiting and discourage people from coming to the hospital. Other hospitals allow even major surgical patients to have a steady stream of visitors from midmorning until eight or nine in the evening.

For the new mother, who is still physically tired from the ordeal of delivery and is trying to make the adjustments to motherhood, a constant trail of visitors can be very taxing and exhausting. While it is great fun to keep showing off the new baby to family and friends, women who have "been there" recommend restraint. The father should spread the word among potential visitors to wait until the baby is at home, or to call first before visiting.

Phone calls are another problem that interferes with rest. Friends should be asked not to call after eight or nine in the evening. If asked, the hospital operator will intercept calls at any hour and ask the callers to try again later. Don't be shy about using the operator's services if sleep is in short supply.

# Rooming-In

"Rooming-In," having the baby in the same hospital room as the mother for all or most of the time, has been increasing in popularity in recent years as a natural outgrowth of the prepared-childbirth experience.

A woman considering rooming-in should investigate the policy of the hospital carefully. Some hospitals have an "all or nothing" policy, which means once the baby is in the room, no matter how tired the mother becomes or how physically uncomfortable the situation may become, the baby is there full-time. Most hospitals prefer what has come to be called "modified rooming-in."

With the modified plan, the mother can keep the baby in her room whenever she desires, for as long as she desires, but when she feels too tired to be responsible for the baby, it can be brought back to the nursery. Most women recommend the modified plan to insure at least a few hours of rest during the night.

Many doctors don't encourage even modified rooming-in. They note that the child will be "rooming-in" for the next seventeen to twenty years and argue that during those first few days the mothers' rest and health are more important than the small amount of bonding or adjusting inherent in the rooming-in process. Parent-child bonding, they say, takes more than two or three days to accomplish. It will take weeks or months once the child is home to truly form that "bond." Right now, at the beginning, the mother needs rest and needs to feel that her carefully spaced moments with the baby are exciting and unique. No study to date has ever shown that rooming-in does anything to help the parents or child adjust and prepare for the realities of life at home when the hospital stay ends.

# The Pediatrician

The new parents and the pediatrician are on the first step of a relationship that will last many years. It is extremely important that they begin to understand each other and feel comfortable about discussing any questions. All expectant parents—or at least mothers-to-be—should consider a prenatal interview with the pediatrician of their choice. The interview is valuable because it provides an introduction to the doctor, so that the person doing that all-important examination of the newborn and reporting to the mother will not be a total stranger. The interview can give the parents a feeling for the doctor, his/her personality and philosophies—and vice versa, for the doctor is also learning something about the attitudes of the parents at the same time.

The interview is a chance to get to see what the doctor is like and for him/her to learn about you. Is this someone with whom you can talk comfortably? Do you agree with his/her attitudes on breast-feeding or working mothers? If a woman plans to go back to work, for example, she should not choose a pediatrician who thinks that is tantamount to irresponsibility or abandoning the child. These general areas of philosophy and personal rapport can be judged during the interview. You will probably want to choose a pediatrician who encourages you to call him/her whenever you have a question, which will almost certainly be often during your child's first few months of life. (But don't call late at night if the question can wait until morning calling hours.)

There are several good ways to choose which pediatrician to contact and, if desired, interview. The best ways are either to ask friends or relatives you trust which pediatrician they use or to ask your obstetrician which pediatrician he/she recommends. You may not be comfortable with the same person, but recommendations are usually an excellent starting point. You will probably find that the pediatrician allots a few hours a week for meeting with parents who want to interview him/her. You may or may not be charged by the physician for the interview time.

Within a few hours after the baby is born, it will be examined by the pediatrician specified by the parents, or the partner of that pediatrician. Babies born during the day will probably be examined before the end of the day. Those born at night are usually examined the next morning during regular rounds unless there are some complications or urgency about the examination.

Thus, the new mother can expect to be visited by the pediatrician while she is eating her breakfast the morning after her delivery and, ideally, every morning thereafter while she remains in the hospital. When talking to the doctor about your child, it can be helpful to think of the baby in parts from head to foot. As you ask questions, start with the head and work your way down. Using this method and writing down your questions in advance will probably help you remember everything you want to discuss.

When interviewed, pediatricians quickly respond that the most important thing new mothers can do is ask questions. They want and expect many questions.

"The first thing I try to do is relieve any anxiety the new mother may have," explained Dr. Richard Lee Zimmern, who has been a pediatrician for thirty years. "Then I try to give her support where she needs it, especially in breast-feeding. After that I try to size up how she feels and how anxious she is. I need her to ask me questions, so I know where she needs the most support. I try to encourage questions and to give helpful answers. At this stage it is very important."

A survey of pediatricians taken in 1980 and 1981 by George Washington University and Howard University researchers found that most pediatricians were eager to discuss crucial issues such as the parents' feelings toward the child and delayed onset of maternal love which bothers so many women, but found that the women were more concerned with the health of the child and getting tips on child care. The women also frequently exhibited anxieties over three issues: "Am I competent to handle the baby?" "Will I be a good mother?" and "Will I be able to nurse effectively?"

Dr. Zimmern and other pediatricians explained that one of the points they try to get across to today's new mother is that motherhood is "on-the-job" training. No one is perfect the first week. All women must gradually build self-confidence in the role.

"I think I see more new mothers today who are anxious about whether they will be competent mothers than I did years ago," said Dr.

Zimmern. "I suppose that's because women today are better educated and read more. But if it were as difficult as they picture it, the human race would have died out a long time ago. It is a lot of work and there is plenty of plain drudgery in being a mother, but each woman will eventually learn to be a capable mother in her own way. It's really the rare woman who does not."

Today, too, pediatricians find an increase in questions about breast-feeding, since many women are opting for nursing. The pediatrician is well-equipped to discuss nursing problems and is concerned because the health of the baby and the mother-child relationship which are both in his/her realm, are involved. The obstetrician, too, can usually advise on nursing because he/she is expert in the hormonal and other physical needs of the mother's body.

Both groups of doctors agree that too often women are reluctant to consult with a doctor about nursing problems, preferring to focus on the baby rather than their own health needs. Whether or not to nurse is completely the decision of the mother, but she should avail herself of all possible sources of help if she has any problems or questions.

No one recognizes better than the baby's doctor that there may be problems in adjustment, both physical and emotional, during the first days or weeks. He/she is experienced in dealing with those problems and, more importantly, expects the issues to arise. New mothers should not be shy about asking questions of the pediatrician, taking his/her time when necessary, whether it be during the first days in the hospital or during the first weeks, months, or years of the child's life.

CHAPTER FOUR
# The First Year

*"I thought motherhood would be a breeze and that everyone else was falling apart because they were neurotic. Then came the realization—Oh, my God, It's another person!" said Monica.*

*"The first time it was just devastating. I was totally unprepared for motherhood. I expected everything was going to be pink lace. Instead I felt inadequate, isolated and incompetent," added Karen.*

When the new parents bring the baby home from the hospital, they are still unaware of the momentous changes that will occur in their lives because they now have a child. There are changes in lifestyle and routine and husband-wife relations which will affect them both, but the woman will be more aware of the differences.

Besides the physiological changes she may experience, she will soon become acutely aware of the fact that she must care for this totally dependent new person around the clock. Not only must she see to the child's every physical need, but she must also provide for its emotional growth. And somehow she must arrange her life so that she is also lover and helpmate to her husband, parent to other children, and a person herself with all her own interests and personal needs fulfilled. Unfortunately, in all probability nothing she has done, nor anything she has studied in high school or college has given her a clue as to where to begin or what to expect.

Certainly the woman who has helped raise younger siblings has some advantages because she knows something about handling a child's physical needs, but even she is completely unprepared for the stunning effect being a mother will have on her, her life, and her priorities.

# The First Days

"I remember the pediatrician warned me that the first few weeks of motherhood would be pure drudgery and I thought, 'How dare he call my child a drudge?' " recalled Laura. "After the first two weeks I knew he had been right."

The first weeks of motherhood are spent learning two things: caring for the child and being comfortable with the child. These are the basics of the job and require mastering new skills one never imagined one might have to perfect.

"It's learning to do all the everyday things that can really confuse you in the beginning," said Rae. "Learning to fold cloth diapers properly or to mix the powdered formulas. Even the snaps on some of the infant stretch suits seem to take an advanced degree to figure out. It is much more of a challenge than you anticipate while you're dreaming about your ideal little baby-to-be."

Even in the best situations, every day will be filled with new skills that must be learned: diapering, bathing baby, taking rectal temperatures, clipping nails on moving fingers and toes, coping with infant hiccups, feeding, burping, making up the crib, dressing the baby properly for weather conditions, and learning to cook and clean with one arm while holding the baby with the other are just a few that will prove to be vital.

In addition, the mother may want to learn a few tricks for her own self-preservation: cleaning a messy diaper without getting ointment caught under her fingernails, anticipating when the baby is about to have a bowel movement or urinate when the diaper is off so that something absorbent can be whisked under the bare bottom within a few seconds, making time for herself even if it means ignoring the baby's cry for a while, and more.

The first few weeks are work. The mother must learn to cope with the child's needs, to read its mind as much as possible, and to become more confident about herself as the caretaker of the child. Unfortunately, there are no black-and-white answers to the many questions of child care, it is very much play-it-by-ear. Every mother must learn to read her own child. In many cases there is no clear measure of good and bad in what the mother chooses to do. One pediatrician added, "The first eight weeks are really hell. But as the woman copes with each day's activities and gradually builds a certain self-confidence about the baby's daily needs, she feels better and more comfortable. Of course, as new problems arise so may additional anxieties in the mother, but at least she knows she has coped in the past and she begins to feel trust in her own judgment and common sense."

Monica mused, "The delivery was a piece of cake compared to what went on for the next two months. You're constantly trying to respond to the baby and you don't know whether you've done the right thing— Did he need diapering, or was he hungry?—and it seems as if the baby wails most of the day."

Part of the adjustment is not only learning to handle all the skills involved in infant care, but learning to feel comfortable and secure being with the child. Some women do find that it takes several weeks before they feel comfortable even holding their newborn, because they have not yet fully accepted the child or the mothering role.

# Nurses vs. Mother or Mother-in-law

About two-thirds of the women studied had some kind of outside help during the first week to two weeks after the baby came home from the hospital. Of these about 60 percent called in their mothers or mothers-in-law, while the rest hired nurses. One woman had her mother come with the first child and a nurse with the second.

There are pros and cons to each form of help. A great deal depends on the personalities involved. Particularly when the home help is to be someone in the family, the prior relationships must be considered seriously before the decision is made. If at all possible, a woman should have some back-up at home during those first days, if for no other reason than to allow her to get some rest. However, if she couldn't get along with the relative before, it won't improve after the baby is present. "Old garbage," as it is called by psychologists, can become magnified with the fatigue and stress during the week of constant contact with the relative. If there are any unresolved conflicts, one should avoid having that relative as a baby aide.

Eighty percent of the women interviewed who had hired nurses were pleased with that choice. Eighty percent who had the baby's grandmother help out felt they had made the right choice for them.

Nurses generally tended to be possessive of the child and often made the mothers feel they had to ask for permission to see their own children. In addition, a few of the women had difficulty adjusting to the nurses' habits. One complained of her nurse's fanatical attitudes toward health foods. The nurse lectured the new parents regularly on their sloppy nutritional habits and cooked only her own special "healthful" meals for the family, which the couple found intolerable. Nurses can sometimes be like sergeant majors. They may try to dominate the mother and father and their guests and intrude into the developing parent-child relationships. Some also make it difficult for older siblings to see the child and begin to get acquainted with the new baby. Nurses may be overly concerned about the germs another child may carry or about overexciting the infant, so they have been known to impede developing sibling relationships.

If an expectant mother plans to have a nurse after the birth, she would be wise to spend some time conducting interviews. No couple should ever call an agency and then accept whomever the agency sends after the child is born. Every couple needs to talk to the nurse in advance and decide if she is right for them. Probably the best way to select a nurse is to interview women who have served as nurses for friends and been especially well-liked. Once a nurse is in the home it is important, too, to remember that the new parents are in charge, not the nurse.

In fact, if a woman has a normal delivery and hospital stay and the infant and mother are both healthy, a nurse may not be the answer. In all probability, a housekeeper who will clean and take care of the husband and other children while the mother takes care of the baby, may really be more to the point. What is really needed is someone to help out so that the new mother can get enough rest.

Mothers (and even mothers-in-law) fared as well as the nurses at providing rest time for the new mother. Every woman who had one of the new grandmothers staying to help with the baby said she was pleased with the extra help she had received. Generally, these women opted to take care of the child themselves and used the resident relative as cook, cleaner, and launderer. This meant that the mothers did not have to concern themselves with any of the household duties and could rest between feedings.

Nurses were better about helping with feedings in the wee hours than relatives. If the new mothers, even the nursing mothers, were willing to allow the nurse to give the infant a bottle in the middle of the night or very early in the morning, they could get some much needed sleep and recover faster from the delivery.

The major complaint voiced about live-in relatives was that they often did not have as good a relationship with the new fathers as with the mothers. Thus, while the new mothers were pleased and often would have liked their helpers to stay longer, the fathers were ready and even eager for their mothers or mothers-in-law to leave.

"I expected to be battling my mother for control," said Ruth, "but instead I was so frazzled I saw her as a help. However, it wasn't all rosy. There was a little friction between my husband and my mother from the beginning."

Conflicts can often arise between new grandmothers, too. Often the live-out grandmother may resent the influence of the assisting grandmother or the bond she sees forming between that grandmother and the child. One new grandmother gave her son so many lectures on how to properly hold his new daughter that he refused to touch the child again until his mother went home. While that fracas was in progress, the other grandmother, not to be outdone, rearranged her daughter's kitchen in the name of helpfulness.

Ina reported some jealousy between her mother and her mother-in-law, who was helping her with the baby. "My mother-in-law is a very soft-spoken, gray-haired lady who is extremely gentle at all times, while my mother has a very loud voice, jet black hair, and a very outgoing manner. She would come in and my daughter would cry and react with fear, probably because of the difference between the two. It really hurt my mother, so my mother-in-law would try to be considerate by closing herself in her room when my parents visited. That would make me feel badly. It was a difficult situation to resolve."

Nurse or mother/mother-in-law is a tricky decision with pitfalls on both sides. Each woman must base the decision on how she gets along with the relative in question (and how her husband does) before making the choice.

# Daddy as Nurse

Rather than bring in a relative or nurse, the child's father may opt to take a week off from work to help out. Depending on his concept of the male role, he may be very useful. He may do the laundry and some housecleaning, shop and even help out with late-night feedings to give the new mother a chance to sleep.

Those women who had the child's father as a helper during the first week or two felt that it worked out well because it made the experience more of a shared, mutual part of their lives. However, they did express a higher level of fatigue than other mothers and commented on their husbands' exhaustion as being greater than expected. The women also found that while the men were helpful, the women were still "in charge" and had to give directions for much of the daily tasks.

The women found that they learned quickly to communicate better with their mates, finding out what the men would and would not do and how much could be divided between them. They also felt it encouraged the men to take an active role in child rearing right from the start and helped the men realize how much work the job of mothering would entail. Perhaps not surprisingly, they also found there was a kind of power struggle during the first weeks—over who would get to play with the new "toy" when it was awake.

# Exhaustion

"Everyone talks about how tired they were the first few months and you figure, 'How tired can I be? I'm used to staying up till the wee hours and then going to work in the morning,'" laughed Karen. "You really don't know what tired means or how tired you can be until you are a parent and you're living through it."

"My parents arrived to help out on the third day the baby was home from the hospital," said Geraldine. "Until then we'd been on our own. We were exhausted. We were so tired that we never even heard the baby cry during the first night that my parents were with us. My parents stayed up with her all night. They never even bothered me to nurse her. In the morning we were so proud of our daughter having slept through and my parents told us we'd been the sleepers. It's a good thing they were there."

The level of exhaustion some women feel becomes overwhelming after a while. They begin to feel as if they cannot cope with the child or their new routine because they are so tired. When the child is cranky or difficult, the exhausted mother has all she can do to keep from strangling the child, a reaction that fills her with guilt and feelings of selfishness. Yet it is a very human response to a highly stressful situation.

"I felt so frustrated," said Brooke. "I remember one night she wouldn't go to sleep. I was rocking her crib mattress, and she was crying and crying. I was so tired and frustrated that I started to shake the mattress so violently she was bouncing up into the air. Then I started to cry because I felt so bad. I kept telling her I was sorry, I didn't mean it."

"I was so exhausted I wasn't sure I even wanted the baby to live," said Kimberly. "One day she fell off her changing table, and for a second I thought she might be dead. I'm ashamed to admit I didn't feel any remorse. I felt as if I had been freed. Of course she was fine and I was glad she wasn't hurt, but for that one instant there was this great sense of relief."

Besides the psychological implications of the constant sense of fatigue, there are also physical problems that can arise. When one is very tired, one also tends to feel less hungry and eat less. In the case of a new mother, especially a nursing mother, nutrition is crucial during the early months.

Nutrition is important for all new mothers, because the body is still healing and because she needs her strength to cope with the stress and activity of infant care. For the nursing mother this is even more important, she is truly "eating for two." What the mother eats is not only supplying her body with nourishment, but is being converted into milk to feed the baby. Yet, because of her fatigue, she tends to eat less than she should to feed both of them. A nursing mother needs 200 to 300 more calories per day than she did when she was pregnant. To increase calorie intake one must eat more. A nursing mother should eat a well-balanced diet and maintain her weight, not lose it. She needs proteins for her own healing and calories for energy and milk production.

Each new mother should establish regular eating and sleeping patterns as soon as possible. A rule all new mothers should commit to memory is "sleep or rest when the baby sleeps." Housework can wait. Sleep, even short naps during the day, is much more important than being able to see your reflection in the polished perfection of the coffee table.

# Feeling Like Yourself

Researchers have found that when asked about what bothered them the most about the first year post partum, more than two-thirds of all women reply that it was the way they looked and the lack of time to take care of their own appearance. In fact, many women complain that they often can't find the time even to bathe or shower for several days. They are too involved in baby care and napping.

"I was embarrassed to have people come over to see the twins because of the way I looked," said Leslie. "There were days when I didn't even comb my hair."

Valerie remembered, "It took almost a year before I felt as if I looked like myself again."

It is very important for the woman's own self-image that she take care of her own needs, whether that be bathing daily, washing her hair, putting on make-up, or manicuring. Yet it is very difficult to learn that the baby can be ignored. If it has been changed, fed, burped, and is in good health, it is really okay to let it cry while mother takes a shower or dries her hair.

Some women have found a compromise that solved the problem. "I can't survive without at least one nice, long bath every day," said Geraldine. "But I found that, no matter what I did to make the baby happy, she always cried the minute I got into the tub. It was as if she had radar and knew. So, I began putting her in the infant seat on the floor next to the tub. She was perfectly happy watching me, and I could sit in the tub as long as I liked."

Faith agreed, "Sometimes I felt as if I was never going to get to bathe in private again. But having an audience was better than no bath at all."

Feeling dirty and unattractive makes a person unhappy with herself and adds to feelings of depression and inadequacy. There must be a time in each new mother's day for herself and her own physical care.

# Breast vs. Bottle

In our grandmother's day, all babies were breast-fed, primarily because there really was no other source of safe nutrition available for infants. Then, in the 1920s, an invention called the icebox changed all that. With the icebox came safe, effective formulas that could be stored at cool temperatures.

What happened next could be called the first women's liberation. Within ten years breast-feeding became passé. Mothers were freed from having to be home with their babies all the time because any available adult could give bottled formula. Rumor had it that formula was better than nursing, and soon virtually a whole generation of women was choosing not to breast-feed their babies.

Then, perhaps ten years ago, Americans became concerned about additives in food, people went "back to nature," and women started nursing babies again to give them a "better," more natural start in life. Today a large number of women choose to nurse their babies. Even working women nurse when home and leave frozen bottled breast milk for babysitters to give the child during the day.

There are pros and cons to both methods of feeding the baby, and they should be examined carefully before making a choice.

**Breast-feeding:** Many women, including those who have nursed one child and bottle fed another, feel this is the easier method. As Estelle put it, "I didn't have to crawl out of bed at 3 A.M. and begin warming up a bottle with a screaming baby in my arms. All I did was bring her into bed with me and give her the breast." However, breast-feeding mothers often have more problems returning to a normal sex life with their husbands than non-nursing mothers because of hormonal and other physical differences (see chapter 6). Breast-fed babies tend to demand feed more often and frequently take longer to sleep through the night.

**Bottle-feeding:** If the baby is bottle-fed, anyone can do the feeding, even at 3:00 A.M.. It is possible to see exactly how much the baby is eating, whereas with breast-feeding judging the amount the baby has eaten involves guesswork and sometimes means the nipple is taken away before the baby has really eaten its fill. But bottle-feeding involves sterilizing bottles, purchasing costly formulas, and wandering around the kitchen at all hours of the night with one eye open, trying to warm the bottle. (While disposable bottle liners eliminate a lot of sterilizing, they are very expensive. Several women mentioned using a microwave oven to warm bottles, at a savings of ten minutes or more.)

The women interviewed who had tried both methods with different children generally preferred breast-feeding because it was easier during the night and because of problems they had had with sterilizing.

Estelle remembered an incident with her second child that convinced her she would nurse any later babies, "I remember once I went out with the baby and his two-year-old brother, and when I reached the shopping center I remembered I had left the sterilizer on the stove. I came rushing home, thinking I would find the house burning down. But I got there in time. It had burned through the bottom of the pot, but had not yet spread."

Deciding whether or not to breast-feed is totally an individual matter and should be based on the needs of the woman. While the bottle gives additional freedom, the breast offers convenience to the mother.

Many women expect breast-feeding to be automatic and easy and are stunned to find that it takes work and some adjustment to nurse successfully. It may take several weeks before the breasts will be comfortable during nursing. The baby's sucking can create pain, cracked nipples, and a lot of self-questioning about whether nursing is for you. In addition, it is difficult to know whether the baby is taking in enough milk during the first weeks. Often the child will nurse for twenty minutes, then doze. An hour later it will awaken screaming from hunger. A particularly sleepy baby may not get enough nutrition during thirty-minute sessions and may begin to lose weight. Most doctors feel the second week is the hardest, because that is when the baby really begins to nurse with energy and the milk has come in fully. It is not unusual for the mother's breasts to become painful and engorged. Many breast-feeding mothers find themselves at the end of the second week exhausted, frustrated, and in pain from nursing. They begin to ask themselves whether this is really what they want to do.

There are some hints for reducing nipple pain in chapter 6. Every nursing mother should also remember that, even if she has opted to nurse, there is no reason why bottles cannot be used for one feeding to allow her additional sleep or why she can't supplement a breast-feeding by offering the baby a bottle after it is finished with the breast.

The La Leche League and other groups that promote breast-feeding often insist that there is something wrong with using the supplemental bottle in addition to nursing. In fact, it may be the salvation of many new mothers. It is often very difficult to tell how much the baby has eaten from the breast. Many children nurse for an hour and then cry hysterically as if they are still hungry. Or, if they do fall asleep, they are awake and crying for food again in two hours. There may be many reasons for this. A woman may not have sufficient milk to fully satisfy the child, or the child itself may not have a mature sucking mechanism. The supplemental bottle at the end of the meal has given many a new mother a needed extra hour of sleep.

"My son was a very hungry baby," explained Ruth. "He cried a lot, and it made me even more anxious about the nursing. I couldn't tell whether he was colicky or hungry. I had been practically ordered by La Leche not to give him a bottle. Later I realized I should have tried a bottle after nursing, because it would have been an excellent test of whether he was hungry. My mother kept saying he was hungry, but, again, La Leche had me so schooled to ignore this kind of 'interference' that I didn't feel free to make an intelligent decision. I gave up trying to nurse at eight weeks.

"However," she continued. "When I had my daughter five years later I remembered that I really had enjoyed the nursing part and had only given it up because of the stress of not knowing why the baby was crying, so I decided to nurse and to prolong each meal by giving her a bottle whenever I needed it. Whenever I felt nervous or unsure of why she was crying I gave her a bottle. I gave her a bottle after nursing quite often. I got a lot more pleasure out of the nursing the second time and

I continued it for six months. I think I really enjoyed the baby more, too."

La Leche can be a good source of information and support for women interested in nursing, but the women interviewed for this study who nursed agreed unanimously that the philosophy advocated by La Leche was too extreme and doctrinaire and did not provide enough of the pros and cons or suggestions for solving problems.

Most doctors feel women should turn to them for answers to nursing problems. The pediatrician is well-equipped to answer many questions and is very concerned that nursing should go well for the sake of the child. The obstetrician can also help from the point of view of the woman's physical reactions and well-being. Every pregnant woman should endeavor to learn more about both forms of infant feeding so she can make the best choice for her own needs, remembering that the decision is hers. Her husband, mother-in-law, or doctor will not be doing the work. It is her body, her breasts, and it is not a decision anyone else can dictate.

# Cloth Diapers vs. Disposables

Disposable diapers have become very popular in the last few years, because they involve no labor on the mother's part except purchasing them and because they don't require pins or rubber pants. There is no question that disposables are simple and easy to use. However, they do have their drawbacks.

They are expensive and there are some mothers who feel they are not as protective as cloth diapers. The disposables without elastic on the legs tend to leak readily, whereas cloth diapers with rubber pants usually do not.

Some mothers have found that younger babies developed severe diaper rashes when wearing the disposables with the elastic leg bands, because so little oxygen could get to their bottoms. Several mothers also commented that the brand which claims to have a deodorizing scent actually develops an atrocious odor when wet.

Of course, cloth diapers are messy. They cannot be just tossed out with the evening trash like disposables. They must be emptied into the toilet bowl and saved for the diaper service. Some services also insist that the parents rinse the diapers out before they will accept them for laundering. You will have to store the dirty diapers for a weekly pickup by the service. If you don't have a garage, basement, or spare bathroom, this can be a problem.

Some women purchase cloth diapers and attempt to launder them at home. This is certainly the least expensive method of diaper care, but there is some question as to whether soap powders or detergents can remove the germs as fully as a diaper-service laundering process can. Needless to say, do-it-yourself diaper cleaning is not for those women who gag at bad smells or the messiest messes.

Again, there are pros and cons to both disposables and cloth diapers, and each woman should consider her priorities carefully before making the decision.

# Illusion vs. Reality

"I expected everything to be pink lace and that I would be a mother like you see on television," explained Karen. "The baby would coo happily, the house would be immaculate, and I would look like I'd just left the beauty parlor every evening. But it wasn't like that at all. I was so frustrated and exhausted, I couldn't even decide what to make for dinner most nights. Larry would come home and find the baby crying, the cat crying, and me crying."

Thanks to the modern media and other fairy tales, many women live under the illusion that once they are married and have a child they will live happily ever after and, except for occasionally scuffed floors or skinned knees, life really can be idyllic.

Within one week after the baby is home the bubble bursts. Unless she has had a nurse or relative helping out, the house has not been cleaned, nothing has been ironed, they are eating pizza or take-out Chinese for dinner, and the entire house smells like one of those white creams used on a baby's bottom (or worse).

As she looks around what was once a neat, reasonably clean home and vows to clean immediately, the baby starts to cry and she runs to respond. Ninety minutes later, after the baby has been fed, changed (at least once), burped and put back to bed, she takes another look at the mess and decides to clean after a short nap. Once again the chores will wait for another day.

Not only is the house a mess, but she may not have even bothered to get dressed. When the baby is three or four months old, she may suddenly look in the mirror and realize she's been wearing the same bathrobe or caftan around the house for weeks and that her hair is unkempt and desperately needs the attention of a beautician. Realistically, if a new mother makes a list of ten things she wants to accomplish during the day, other than baby care, and manages to do two or three, she rates an A+.

This is hardly what she had imagined. Because of her preconceived idea of what life with baby would be, a woman begins to doubt herself when the inevitable deterioration of her home begins. She feels she must be inadequate because she cannot handle everything with ease. She may have held a responsible managerial position before having a baby, kept the house clean and cooked gourmet meals most nights, too. Yet now suddenly throwing two lamb chops into the broiler is an organizational problem of enormous magnitude.

The causes are complicated. Fatigue, the residual shock to the system of the delivery process, preoccupation with the baby, and difficulties adjusting to a new schedule and new responsibilities are probably among the leaders.

Having a baby in the house is a bigger adjustment than most people realize. Just the hours and care it takes to handle the baby are enough to throw the best of us. And no one has an adequate advanced education. All new mothers are learning day by day. Few, if any, women have the mythical "maternal instinct" that automatically selects the right response to a baby's cry or the right solution to a new problem.

"I remember one day when the baby was a few weeks old I didn't know what was bothering her, and my husband said, 'Use your mother's intuition.' I realized that I didn't have any and I thought that was strange. Of course, now I know nobody else has it either," laughed Mona.

Not only do many women expect too much from themselves because of an unrealistic picture of what a mother should be, but many don't have any idea what to expect from the child, so they are constantly concerned about whether the child is normal.

They report having asked the doctor if the child was blind because he was having trouble focusing (a normal condition for babies), and genuinely not knowing what pace of physical development and awareness to expect from the child. Many said they were surprised at how often the baby cried or how little it slept or how much it slept.

Research done at the University of Washington indicated that a startlingly large number of women did not have any idea when their babies could see (they see from birth), when they could follow objects and faces with their eyes or voices by turning their heads, or at what point they would become aware of inanimate objects around them. Most babies are sensitive to these stimuli at birth, yet more than a third of the mothers questioned thought it wouldn't happen until the children were at least two months old. In fact, four-day-old babies have been taught to turn their heads at the sound of a buzzer and by two weeks seem to know their mothers quite well.

Since many women do not know what to expect from a child, they are entering a new world without any guidebook, only a few collected, but probably idealized, pictures created by the media or grandma's recollections of what her children were like . . . stories that have become happier and more loving as the years have gone by.

It doesn't take long before a new mother realizes she is not the every-hair-in-place, calm, cheerful, beautiful, and completely organized television wonder mother, but a tired, disorganized baby-care machine yearning for the quiet of days past (a feeling she may not fully lose until she is a grandmother herself!).

# Worry, Worry, Worry

"We both became real nuts," said Heather. "We'd see a story on televison about a baby with bubonic plague in India and we'd worry about something happening to our baby."

The birth of a healthy, normal baby does not relieve the nervousness many couples feel about whether they will have a happy, healthy child. If anything, it creates a new level of anxiety. New parents listen often to hear if the child is still breathing. Women even reported stopping in the middle of making love to listen for the baby's even breathing. The publicity about the Sudden Infant Death Syndrome (SIDS) has been so effective in recent years that many parents are overly alert for it.

Then there is the daily question of whether the child has been dressed properly for the weather. Pediatricians explain that if the parent is comfortable, the baby is comfortable. Babies do not need to be bundled up and overheated. Put as much clothing on the baby as you put on yourself.

"It got so that I hated taking him anywhere," said Erica. "Even in the supermarket people would come up to me and say he was overdressed or underdressed and I was already confused enough."

Some women reported that every time they walked down the steps carrying the child they were afraid they would drop the child. What might happen? The baby drank from the dog's water dish. Will she be poisoned? Irrational fears of all kinds begin to creep up on the unsuspecting parents. Any slight deviation can cause anxiety or panic.

The simple things are often the most challenging, and new parents tend to go to the pediatrician at the slightest cause.

Geraldine recalled: "When the baby was three weeks old I ran some errands leaving her with her father. When I returned, she was napping and he was panic-strickened.

"As I walked in the door he rushed up to me hysterical that there was some 'white stuff' coming out of her ears. I tried to reassure him by saying she had begun cheesing those curdled white gobs babies are famous for the day before. He insisted that what he had seen was not cheesing because he would have recognized cheesing and that something was really wrong with her. I examined her and saw nothing, but he nagged until I called the doctor.

"Of course it was cheesing since nothing could possibly have been pouring out her ears, and I felt humiliated that I had been bullied into calling the doctor, but the doctor was as nice as could be. I guess he had received similar calls from parents in his years of practice."

A father of a twelve-year-old still recalled vividly his first panicky moment as a parent: "When Jon was two weeks old the baby nurse we had pointed out to us that there was a small lump on his lower stomach. The nurse could not identify it.

"My wife, who had had a very difficult delivery and was just beginning to get around, started to shake all over. I felt my stomach knot. Could we have a defective child?

"We rushed to the pediatrician. I went in with the baby, because my wife was too weak to face watching the examination. The doctor studied him carefully and then muttered something about this being a classic case and that he wanted all his office staff to see. I can't even describe how sick I felt.

"When the nurses came in the doctor announced that Jon had a classic case of an as yet undescended testicle. When the child was laying down there was a lump in his belly. When you held him up it disappeared because the testicle fell into place.

"I was so relieved that I ran out to the waiting room to tell my wife, leaving the baby with the doctor. Of course, in the normal course of growth, the testicle dropped and was never any problem to him. But what a scare we gave ourselves!"

According to pediatricians, they receive dozens of phone calls daily from new mothers. Most of the time the questions are trivial, but the answers reassure nervous mothers. "We'd rather have them feel comfortable calling us and get the right answer than become panicky," said one pediatrician. "I never consider a call from a parent during the first years a nuisance, no matter how minor the problem."

Nerves are just a part of being a responsible parent. Welcome to the club!

# Is My Mind Going?

Many women find during the first few months of motherhood that they begin to feel as if their intelligence quotient has dropped significantly. They are forgetful and can't do simple things they did without thinking before the baby came. Even remembering her best friend's husband's name can be a test worthy of a final exam for a new mother. She will certainly feel a loss of control and great frustration from this sudden incompetence on her part.

Actually, this forgetfulness and new fallibility is a perfectly natural reaction to the fatigue, stress, and distractions of new motherhood. Every new mother goes through a period in which she is so physically and mentally exhausted and so completely focused on the baby and everything the baby does that she is only partially aware of other details.

GARLAND COUNTY
COMMUNITY COLLEGE
LIBRARY
Hot Springs, AR 71901

"I remember when the baby was a few weeks old, my husband suddenly realized he had no clean suits for work," said Randi. "He asked me why I hadn't taken the suits to the cleaners. I told him he hadn't asked me to. He insisted that he had and that his lack of clean clothing was my fault. We started screaming at each other, having the most ridiculous argument about whether or not he asked me to have his suits cleaned. I honestly don't recall him ever asking me to clean his suits, but I was so 'out of it' for weeks that I suppose it is perfectly possible he did and it just didn't register in my mind at all."

# Friends and Relatives

One of the obligations that arrives with the baby is the regular stream of friends and relatives who will want to take a close look at the new baby, to bring gifts and good wishes. It would be rude to turn them away, and in many ways their visits are fun and something to which most women look forward. However, there are pros and cons to all the visitations and friendly gestures.

Visitors can be helpful by bringing food for dinner during your first days home or calling first to see if there is an errand they can run on the way to see you. A thoughtful visitor also knows when to leave and not overtax the new mother.

Visitors can also be a bit of a pain. Donna remembered that when her daughter was a few days old her sister visited with her three young children. "It would have been fine if she'd stayed for an hour and left," Donna recalled, still expressing anger at an event which had occurred many months before. "But she stayed all day and her youngest, who is about three, made a mess of my kitchen and no one bothered to clean it up. When she arrived we were exhausted from being up during the night with the baby, and by the time she left we were on the verge of collapse. But we had to clean up the trash that was all over the kitchen before we could go to sleep. You'd think she would have known better."

Donna confided that after her sister's visit she found a trick for controlling visitors. "When people want to come to see the baby, they're either going to get insulted or think there's something wrong with the child if you just give a flat 'No,' " she cautioned. "But I found that if I said, 'Well, she's a little colicky today. I wish you'd wait to see her when she's really at her cutest,' people would decide not to come that day. If I was really worn out or just wasn't up for visitors that's what I did, and it worked like a charm."

Another part of having visitors is that everyone tries to help by offering advice, and frequently the advice is contradictory. What worked for Gert made Hilda's child hysterical.

"You'll go crazy if you try to listen to all the advice," laughed Monica. "I heard more stories of what to do in given situations than I could even remember and begin to repeat."

Shelley agreed: "I remember when one of my aunts discovered that my two-month-old was receiving only breast milk to eat. She assured me that the child would not grow without several ounces of tomato juice daily. Have you ever heard of a two-month-old drinking tomato juice? And that is just one piece of advice friends or relatives offered.

"One will say the baby's room must be warm. The next one to visit will open the windows and insist in must be cool. If the baby is being fussy one aunt will say he's hungry, the next will say he has gas from being overfed. You learn not to listen after a while."

Relatives, in particular, have a tendency to bypass the parents and head straight for the child like bees to honey. They will say things like, "We came to see the baby. Of course, we want to see you, too." Many women have taken offense at the offhanded way they are treated.

"I feel like a discarded old shoe," said Devon. "For nine months they all doted on me, and now it's like I'm an also-ran. My mother-in-law doesn't make any bones about it."

In a few cases, well-meaning brothers, sisters, and in-laws moved in with the couple to "help." "We had quite a crowd at my house when I got home from the hospital," said Leslie. "We lived in the Midwest and our parents lived on either coast, so once they came they stayed with us. When I got home my parents and sister and Rick's brother and mother were all camped out in the living room. It was quite a gathering, and it didn't end for a week.

Many couples decide to take care of all the cousins and friends in one swoop by having a large party so everyone gets to see the baby at once. This can be a useful device if it is handled properly and doesn't get out of hand. Several women reported that having relatives visit in groups of ten or fifteen for simple Sunday brunches or dessert one evening was very satisfactory, but larger gatherings often upset the family routine too much.

# Christenings, *Bris Milahs*, and Other Rituals

Along with the concept of parties for the family to introduce the child go the gatherings surrounding christenings, *bris milahs,* baby namings, and other new-baby-related events that may bring large numbers of people together expecting to be fed and entertained by the new parents.

Normally christenings and baptisms occur several weeks after the child is born, as do baby naming parties. But the Jewish rite of circumcision, the *bris milah* (commonly called the bris), occurs when the child is eight days old. With all due respect to religious custom, virtually every Jewish woman interviewed who held a bris for a newborn son reported that either she or her husband was very ill the following day. The combination of lack of sleep with the stress and added fatigue of entertaining and organizing the bris took its toll in every case.

Women who had held brises for two sons, reported that, indeed, one of them had become ill after the first because they had not rested, but had overdone the role of host or hostess. Two or three years later, when the second son came along, they knew better. The fathers did less and the mothers stayed in bed and let guests come in to see them, in small groups.

Christening parties and other large gatherings held when the baby was a number of weeks old were not so exhausting for the parents. In fact, many said working on the plans was good for them because it distracted them from constant focus on the child itself and gave them something to do together. However, several described family arguments over menus and cooking chores.

Keeping parties and the extra work that comes with them to a minimum the first few months is excellent advice that all new parents, eager as they are to show off their perfectly wonderful new child, should heed.

# Visiting the Pediatrician

When the baby is about two weeks old, and regularly thereafter, the child should be taken to the pediatrician for a checkup and innoculations. A small number of children are delightful at the doctor's office, cooperate fully, don't cry and make it an uneventful experience. However, the majority of young children make the trip to the pediatrician a true trial for their mothers. They cry, kick, urinate on both the mother and doctor. Some even have to be held still by the parent in order to be examined.

Most parents do not know what to expect on that first visit to the pediatrician, so they come unprepared. The more experienced parents know to bring extra diapers, ointment, and even a change of clothing. (Some doctors keep disposable diapers in the examining rooms since they know that the child's diaper must be removed for a complete examination, but some do not.) A bottle of formula or sugar water (if the mother prefers) may be needed if there is a long wait to see the doctor. A newborn is too young to appreciate the toys and books in the office, but might be more comfortable during a waiting period if it is allowed to lie flat in a traveling infant bed (the quilted basket-like bassinets that have become popular in recent years for infant travel), not held. You might also want to take a friend or relative along to hold the child after the exam so you are free to talk to the doctor and ask all your questions.

If you find there is a long wait and do not want your newborn exposed to the colds and viruses of sick children in the waiting room, ask the nurses to find you somewhere away from the other children to wait. Most pediatricians instruct their staff to provide such assistance to well babies, but the mother usually must ask.

# Restaurants and Other Travels

"Going out or traveling with kids is tough," said Holly. "In restaurants you have to bring along some baby food for them to eat.

Then they spit up and other people stare at you for causing a disturbance. And you always have to have a diaper bag. It's amazing how much planning goes into just going to Grandma's for the day."

Despite the argument many people will give as they claim restaurants and hotels are no place for children, many couples try to go out to dinner or go on vacation with their infants. Some restaurants have a high chair or booster seat, and younger babies can sit (or even nap) very happily in their infant seats while the parents enjoy their meal. However, it does take planning and some getting used to, and you should call ahead to be sure the restaurant has the seats and welcomes children.

"I always kept a beach-sized towel in my car," said Vikki. "So, if a diaper had to be changed while we were in a restaurant, I would run back out to the car, spread the towel on the seat and change her there."

Women have described having to run into a nearby store to buy a new outfit for the child when the one the child was wearing became soiled with urine or feces and they were too far from home to make that trip feasible. (Moral: always carry an extra outfit for the child.) Traveling anywhere involves more equipment—a car seat, of course, a stroller, diaper bag, perhaps a favorite toy or two to keep the child happy.

Many nursing mothers are embarrassed by nursing in public (and others may be embarrassed by the nursing mother), so a bottle of formula or juice might be as essential for them as for a non-nursing mother.

Several women reported no problem traveling with newborns and believed that getting away with their husbands and the baby when it was only a few days old had been excellent therapy for them, but most described a great deal of work, extra effort, and planning that went into even the smallest trip with young children.

# Limits

Not only travel and restaurant outings, but every aspect of a woman's life can become more limited by the arrival of the child. In fact, the early weeks are probably less restricting than the later months can become.

While the new infant is very absorbing, many women find themselves feeling "trapped" or at least confined, rarely getting out. A newborn who isn't a frequently crying baby can be very accommodating. It will sit and watch Mommy do her daily routine, bathe or watch TV, happy to get some attention and have lots of external stimuli to study. During the first three or four months when the child still cannot roll away or crawl or climb out of things, a mother can still cook or do other mandatory things with a well-fed and burped baby as an observer.

However, when the baby begins to move on its own, life changes once again. Wriggling babies who can crawl away do not sit well at club meetings or card games, nor can mother take her eye off the child even in the confines of the bedroom.

"I think I had a delayed adjustment to the baby when she was about six months old," explained Jenny. "When she was three months, if I was busy or just plain exhausted, I could just hold her or put her down on the bed and she'd watch me. She'd even watch me sleep. When she reached about six months everything changed. Now I have to be 'on' all the time, no matter how exhausted I am. She isn't the little bundle I can put down on the couch beside me while I watch soap operas."

This change sneaks up on parents, seemingly happening out of the blue one day. Mothers described how it had become their habit to leave the child in the middle of the bed while straightening the room and the baby laid there unmoving, until one day, when the mother's back was turned, it rolled over several times and plunged to the floor. They mentioned watching a previously immobile child suddenly roll off the sofa before the startled parents could react.

Once that happens, the mother begins to find she cannot stray more than a few feet from the child unless it is asleep or in a crib or playpen. As involved with the child as she was before, she now has become a watchdog and bodyguard.

More equipment enters the scene: an infant walker, gates for the stairs, perhaps a harness to keep the child in the highchair or stroller. Now, too, it has become more difficult for mother to find time to bathe or primp herself. Probably when the baby is napping she will collapse, too. After all, her day is even more active than the baby's.

Not only is life more limited during the day, but most couples find parenthood limits their evening life, too. Fully 90 percent of the people interviewed said they went out less at night than before the baby came. The reasons they mentioned were fatigue, the cost of sitters, and unwillingness to leave the baby too often. Although many commented that they went out at least once a week for dinner, more commented that they went out less and tended to make dinners out getting pizza or eating at a family restaurant where they could take the baby comfortably.

# Becoming "Boring"

One of the most common comments heard among mothers of infants and toddlers is the fear that they are becoming "boring" because they don't do interesting things and therefore don't have exciting or intellectually stimulating things to discuss. Mostly, they fear, they just talk about the baby.

Cassie became quite down on herself because of her self-perceived "boringness." "I had had an exciting job as a fashion coordinator, and then suddenly I was a mother with nothing to do but care for the baby. I tried to find a mothers' group, but the conversations were so trite. We'd sit around talking about diarrhea and the babies' bedtimes. My husband would tell me about his fascinating day, and all I'd have to report was how many bottles the baby had had during the day. Then I found myself watching soap operas for the first time in my life and I was sure I had become the ultimate dull housewife."

For the woman who worked prior to having a child that concept, "I started watching soap operas," seems to become a trigger for fears of growing dullness and intellectual decline. Eighty percent of the women interviewed who had previously worked specifically commented that they knew they were in a rut and had become "boring" when they started watching afternoon soap operas regularly.

About half decided to combat this terrible syndrome by reading newspapers and watching the eleven o'clock news so they could be "informed." "After a few weeks of that I realized I had never cared about the news before, so the whole effort was silly," said Erica. "All I accomplished was making myself more tired because I wasn't getting to bed until 11:30."

While some women found being at home with the baby boring and depressing, more found the first five or six months to be a pleasant diversion and made the best of it by telling spontaneous jokes about diaper changing, mealtime, or other daily events.

# The "Formerly Working Woman"

Women who worked for any length of time, especially those who were successful in responsible careers, seem to have the most difficult adjustment to being at home, even when they have given up work of their own choice because they genuinely want to be a full-time parent.

Most working women do not appreciate how difficult child/home care is until they experience it themselves. During the years they were working they thought women who stayed at home had it easy. "Before I had a baby I'd think, What do these women have to complain about? All they have to do is take care of the house. They don't have to be in court prepared to argue a case at nine tomorrow morning. They have no responsibility except the house. Now I know they were under just as much pressure as I was," said Jenny.

Many working women think that what their homemaker counterparts do all day takes little effort. Then these smug, competent executive-type women have children and they discover it wasn't so simple and they now have as much or more responsibility than they did when they were working. They are responsible for a helpless child, a home, meals, and an array of details and issues they never thought about before.

The first reaction may be a sense of inadequacy and disappointment in themselves. "I felt like a total failure," said Karen, a former marketing executive. "I couldn't make the simplest decision. Here I was this competent woman who had been making so much money, and I fell apart. I couldn't handle the situation. I was sure I was inadequate. I couldn't keep up the house. I couldn't do the laundry. I couldn't cook. In short, I was totally unprepared for new motherhood and just devastated by the responsibility."

In addition, many formerly working women found they had become used to getting out with great freedom. Lunches with friends or co-workers had been a regular and enjoyed part of their lives, but one doesn't run out to lunch often with a new baby. They begin to feel cut off from the world, from their friends, and from the ego satisfaction they got from excelling at their jobs.

"I made the conscious decision not to return to work until the children were in school," said Anna. "But it hasn't been easy. It was difficult to adjust to being in the house. I had imagined that I would keep very active. I'd just grab the baby and go, go, go, but realistically that just doesn't happen. At first I felt being a housewife was degrading, but I don't anymore. I work hard here at home. I keep the house clean. I do everything for the baby and my husband that needs to be done, and I do things on the side for myself, too."

Echoing Anna, virtually every woman who had worked in a career said she felt being identified as a housewife was degrading, at least during the first year post partum. It was a big ego-blow to be identified by that dirty word.

"Whenever I have to fill out a form that asks my employment and I have to say homemaker or housewife I still flinch," said Mona, a systems analyst who did work for a few months after her daughter was born, but gave it up to stay home with the child. "But worse than that is when people refer to you as Charles's wife or Hildy's mother, as if you no longer have an identity of your own. I still have difficulty with that."

In many of the problems and awakenings that occur in the first year post partum are roots of varying levels of depression which will be examined more thoroughly in chapter 8.

# CHAPTER FIVE
# The Couple

*"His idea of a perfect wife is one who takes care of the kids, keeps a nice house, plants flowers around the outside, and that's not my idea at all. When the baby came, the bottom of our relationship fell out because of a lack of communication," Mona explained.*

*"I think having children really strenghtened our marriage. I had spent so many years being jealous of all the time he put into the business, and now I have the kids to fill my time. It kind of makes up for it. We're both glad," said Nancy.*

The birth of a child is an extremely powerful event that makes permanent changes in the lifestyle, relationship, and attitudes of the couple. Parenthood affects the way one looks at one's self, one's spouse, other family relationships, and the world in general.

Studies by sociologists and psychologists have repeatedly indicated that those couples that had the most cohesive marital bond and healthy open communications as part of their marital relationship adjusted most easily to the first few months—the transition period—of parenthood.

If communication is good between the couple, parenthood, while still an adjustment, may not become a crisis, since both will feel able to express needs and be sensitive to the needs of the other. This applies not only sexually, but in all areas of their relationship.

If the communication in the relationship was bad or non-existent before the baby came, it won't improve after birth. If her complaint has always been that she doesn't know what he wants or that she has difficulty telling him what she wants, then they have a problem in their relationship that will be magnified in many respects by the complications of the post partum period. When one adds the already existing gaps to the fatigue and stress that normally follow the birth of an infant, then whatever subtle anger she may have had before may very well rise to the surface.

Many women spoke of becoming angry at little things that might never have bothered them before. They used the term "grouchy" for their own attitude toward their husbands' little foibles and spoke of arguing a great deal until they were able to improve their ability to communicate. Often the irritation seemed linked to her feeling that he expected her to continue to serve him in the same manner she had prior to the baby's arrival.

Anna said, "Before the baby I'd jump at his every wish. Afterward I had too much to do. If I had to choose between his cry and the baby's I went to the baby, and we'd argue about it. He'd get furious and storm out. It took us weeks to work it out."

"I became bitchy and grouchy after a few weeks at home," added Ina. "I had been a career woman before the baby, and afterward I felt like a housewife or a servant. I took care of the baby, my husband, and the chores. I was unbearable. But fortunately we do have a close, open relationship and I was able to talk it out and realize where the problem was."

If the communication is good, as in Ina's case, each can become aware of the other's needs. He will understand her fatigue and the emotions she is facing in her new role. They will be able to work together to see to mutual needs.

Research has indicated that couples who are together longer before the baby comes usually have developed a better system of communication and methods for smoothing over conflict. While this is not an absolute and it can often be more difficult for a couple with set patterns to make the adjustment into parenthood with all the changes that creates in their lives, the evidence is that couples who wait do fare better. Reseachers have found that couples who do not rush into having a baby, but wait a few years, generally adjust with less stress.

# The Issues

## Responsibility

To suddenly be totally responsible for the life and well-being of a tiny infant who is completely incapable of doing anything for himself is an awesome realization. It is unfortunate that parenthood, possibly the most crucial and intense occupation for human beings, is the only one which our society still leaves to non-professionals. Parenthood, especially first-time parenthood, is the realm of the well-meaning amateur.

The suddenness of the onset of parenthood serves to accentuate the lack of professional training from which virtually all new parents suffer. In every other field of endeavor, be it education, a job, or even marriage, there is a "honeymoon" period, a trial time in which one learns the duties by trial and error and acquires the skills needed to be successful.

Parenthood is the only exception. A helpless, and probably demanding, baby is born and given to the parents to nurture. Even if they have taken a prepared-childbirth class and read a few books, they probably have little or no knowledge of what this responsibility really entails. And it is a role with no vacations or breathers until the child is an independent adult (and some would argue not even then!)

In motherhood a woman becomes a competitor with other women, including her mother and grandmother, whom she may have idealized. All the education, intelligence, beauty or savoir-faire she has may not give her an edge in this test. And she has an overwhelming responsibility to be perfect, or as near perfect as she can be. In fact, experts feel today's "liberated" women are even more highly motivated to be "perfect" mothers than their less liberated counterparts.

Even if a woman continues to work and mothering is not what she does for most of her day, the message of past generations is clear. She must still strive to be the most complete, perfect mother she can be. Yet being a mommy is boring. Many women find themselves frustrated, anxious, and uncomfortable in the role. Through their entire lives they saw their own mothers as confident and as a source of security for them. Now they find out their mothers were probably as scared, unsure, and bored as they are.

Added to the feelings of competition and surprise, the responsibility for this infant can become a major issue for even the most competent, self-assured people. Women who had worked as successful professionals in fields such as law, health care, sales and marketing confessed their weaknesses when confronting the responsibility of caring for the child. They felt like babies again themselves, turning to their husbands for assistance and cooperation more than ever before in their marriage.

"I always prided myself on being strong," said Jenny, an attorney. "But since the baby came, Brad has had two babies to deal with. There are times, especially when she is sick, that I find myself calling him and begging him to come home from work to help me. There isn't really that much he can do, but I need the support. I need to know I'm doing the right thing."

"I had had a very responsible job, but when the baby came I felt incompetent," added Karen, a former marketing executive. "I couldn't make the simplest decision concerning the baby without calling either the doctor or Larry. I was on the phone with one or the other at least twice a day."

Not only was this new responsibility a crisis for them, but many women felt demeaned by their sudden need to lean on their husbands. All the self-esteem they had developed through their success in other fields seemed to float away as they began to see themselves as weak and dependent women because of their responses to motherhood. They began having doubts about themselves as persons and mothers.

The need to share responsibility for the baby is a common and understandable reaction. Especially with a first baby, when there is so much for the new mother to ingest and master, she is likely to feel overwhelmed and want her husband to share the burden and some of the anxiety over the constant decision making. She is not asking to be consoled so much as to be told she has made the right decision and is doing the right thing. At the same time, however, she is putting new, greater demands on her husband, who probably is overwhelmed by his new responsibilities as a father.

Men tend to react a bit differently from women, since traditionally women handle the day-to-day home care in Western families. A man may become more conscious of his duty to perform and achieve in the working world to support his growing family. At the same time that he is trying harder to advance at work and promote his career, his wife phones him twice a day to consult on baby foods and sniffles, often interrupting important meetings.

While he probably wants to be consulted and to be kept abreast of every clever new thing his child has done, he becomes torn. Besides the interruptions being a potential problem for him on the job, the fact that Junior bit the dog may not seem as important a closing the deal that could lead to a good promotion. In addition, the father doesn't want to be overwhelmed by parental responsibilities anymore than the mother, so his inclination to put a business deal before a home crisis can be a form of denial of the responsibility, a way for him to escape a little.

The friction that may build because of conflicts which develop for both the new mother and the new father can become a real problem in their relationship and in their relationship with the child if they cannot communicate and explain their feelings.

# Nurturing

Besides finding that she needs to be reinforced as a capable decision maker and responsible caretaker for the helpless infant in her charge, the woman may find that her need to be nurtured and stroked is greater than before she became a parent.

All of us need nurturing during our day. We enjoy hearing how attractive we look or what a good job we did on our work assignment. Instead of being told how intelligent she is or what a tasteful wardrobe she has acquired, she probably needs to be told that she is a good mother. She could measure her success on the job because there were tangible results, but how does one measure the success of motherhood when the infant is three months old and cries most of its waking hours? The only measure she has is what is said to her and, most importantly, what she hears from her husband. Women experience a great deal of anxiety with a child, especially a first child, and they need to be told they have passed the "mother" test.

Many women also see themselves as cows during the first weeks or months. Their figures have not come back, they may be overweight, and, if they're nursing, their breasts may be huge. Yet most women need to know that they are sexy and that their husbands still love them as much, or better, than the child. He comes home a 6:30 or 7:00 P.M. and she has been waiting with bated breath since noon for adult companionship and some emotional stroking. Then he rushes in the door and bypasses her on the way to see the baby. The mother is not getting the positive stroking she needs. She begins to feel isolated. Now, not only is she overwhelmed by the tremendous responsibility of parenthood, but she feels she is not being complimented as a woman. It is all too easy for couples to slip into this pattern. This problem may arise because he doesn't know what she wants him to do: he may think it will please her if he shows enormous affection for the child when he comes home. Also, she has been part of his life for a while and the baby is new. He may perfectly naturally want to be with the baby.

In a good marriage, with free-flowing communications, expressing the feelings that are building can help. Asking what the other person needs before the problem begins to develop is a good way to avoid some potential difficulties.

# Anger

Popular myths have it that, despite a little fatigue and perhaps some uncertainty about which disposable diapers to use, women are automatically blissfully happy after they have their babies. Now the woman is fulfilled! What could she possibly have to be unhappy or angry about?

However, many women reported growing feelings of anger at both their husbands and their situations as weeks of being home with the baby turned to months. In particular, the women who had been the happiest and most successful in their jobs prior to the arrival of the baby often were ready to explode after spending most of their time trapped at home with an infant for many months. When that happens, the feelings can fester into anger at the husband or at the situation.

"I had worked in a very nice job for thirteen years," said Ina, a former executive secretary. "I willingly gave it up to stay home, but after a while I began to feel I was missing something. I became very demanding of my husband. I would snap at him for not doing enough. I realized I was angry because I wasn't doing as much as I used to. It took me a while to adjust to staying home and being a full-time mother."

"I was so bored with being in the house and tired from not getting much sleep," remembered Ruth. "I was full of conflicts. I became very angry . . . not at Joe directly, but at the situation and at the baby. I was just furious at our whole way of life. Then I became angry at the way I looked and at almost everything."

Another cause of anger may be the roots of the pregnancy itself. Why a woman got pregnant often is a factor in how well she adjusts to the role. Unfortunately, not every child comes into this world because its parents planned for and wanted to have a child at that moment in time. If a woman feels she was talked into having a child by her husband or impregnated because he failed to use a contraceptive or if the pregnancy was accidental, she may be harboring a conscious or subconscious resentment of him.

During the difficult first weeks of parenthood her resentment may blossom into raging anger as she sees him free to come and go as before while she sits home with the baby. On top of that, she may have some physical discomfort as a result of the pregnancy or may not have any sex drive while he is as eager as ever, both of which could be reasons for her to be even more resentful of his relative freedom.

Whatever negative aspects there may be to being a woman may be exaggerated in her mind, increasing her anger. One woman complained bitterly that women had to endure all the pain while men got all the fun. "We have menstrual cramps, pain with the first attempts at intercourse, pain with childbirth and pain afterward . . . they just have fun," she ranted, venting months of pent-up anger.

Another described becoming increasingly angry as she watched her husband coming and going as always. "He goes to work and I sit at home. Then he has softball and racquetball and professional society meetings. I feel angry, and yet I don't want to deny him a few pleasures. It's difficult," she intoned.

Unfortunately, as the wives get angrier and more unhappy, the husbands tend to react by finding more excuses to be away, aggravating the situation even further. Facing the issue and coping with it is the only way to begin to ease those feelings and solve the problem.

"I found it depressing and irritating to always be around the house," added Ruth, a social worker. "I probably was taking it out on Joe all the time because I began to realize that he would use any excuse to get out of the house for a few minutes. I'd say we were low on milk and he'd fly out the door to the store. Finally I began to argue with him to let me go while he stayed with the baby. That led to our having a discussion of his behavior and my feelings, and we found we were able to laugh about it and compromise. We both felt a lot better afterward."

# Our Baby/My Baby

Most couples enter the pregnancy and participate in a prepared-childbirth experience because they are hoping to share and jointly enjoy the childbirth process, but once the child is here, one or both may lose track of the fact that it is "their baby" and begin to feel that it is "my baby" or "your baby." Parents often tease about the baby's being "my baby" when it is good and "your baby" when it is bad, but while that does go on at a superficial level, it can sometimes be a much deeper and potentially damaging feeling.

As one woman expressed it: "When the baby was about two months old, I decided I wanted to divorce my husband so I could have the baby all to myself." She was not alone. In fully one-quarter of all the cases examined, one of the parents developed a disproportionate attachment to the child, to the exclusion of the other parent.

Brooke described not trusting her husband, a doctor, to do anything for the baby: "Tom tried to be helpful, but nothing he did was right," she explained. "I had to do everything. When he would do anything for her, I would find fault with it and I'd yell at him to stay away, that he was doing it wrong. He stopped trying to help and felt very left out."

Many women begin to look upon the infant as a little girl might her first baby doll—this is mine, not ours. The "my baby" versus "our baby" syndrome is pathological. Parenthood should be something done together, not an exercise in possession by either party.

It is not always the mother who develops an exaggerated attachment to the baby. Often it is the father. A father can become overly involved with his new son, his "heir" and all that role may entail in his mind. Or, he may feel that a daughter needs extra fathering to protect her from the cruel world.

"After the baby was born I often questioned my relationship with my husband," Heather admitted. "The baby was so much in focus for him. He has two daughters by a previous marriage, but this was his son and it took on an overwhelming importance for him. This was his boy, and it looked just like him. Some of my friends suggested that I should feel bad because Jeff was loving me through the baby and not for myself, but I don't care. As long as he is happy and loves me, I don't care why."

Nancy sketched a similar picture. "I think it's obvious that Mike is much more attached to his son than his daughter," she explained. "Of course they look exactly alike, but it's more a sense of the baby's being his replacement. He spends much more time with him than he did with our daughter. He's never voiced it, but I know just by watching him. It's his son."

Often the husband gets a feeling of "her baby" because of the obvious mother-child attachment, especially if the woman is nursing. He can feel excluded, even though she may not mean for him to and may genuinely want to share the parenting process with him. Perhaps Jenny expressed it best of the women who described the process: "Brad has admitted feeling left out by the breast-feeding. I can understand why, because it is a very special kind of thing. I could really see it and feel for him last week when the baby was ill with a virus. There is a mother-to-child bond that has formed. Last week she was quite sick. He wanted so much to be the one to comfort her, but all she wanted was for me to hold and cuddle her. He looked so forlorn, I felt terrible for him. I know he sometimes feels a little left out."

A man may openly wish he could take the infant to his own breast so he could experience the bond and parental strength inherent in nursing. Many men have openly admitted they are jealous that their wives can nurse while they cannot. They are jealous of the strong attachment that grows between the mother and the child during the nursing process and the fact that it is the mother upon whom the child becomes dependent. The addition of the baby into the little family group causes feelings and relationships to be adjusted and rearranged much more than most expectant couples can really anticipate.

The rearrangement of the relationships can be described as going from two confluent lines to a triangle. Each of the parents has a major job defining the shape and dimensions of the triangle over the next few years, but especially during those first months when all the fluctuating emotions and confused feelings are trying to form into a true love for the child and a continued healthy, loving relationship with one's spouse. The baby erases forever the two-person pair and creates a permanent triangle that will affect their lives on all levels: emotional, psychological, and physical.

Now the couple must share their love not only with each other, but with this tiny new partner. That can be stressful for some people. For example, a woman who is feeling inadequate or insecure because of her post partum appearance may become more insecure emotionally if she perceives her husband as loving the baby more than he does her. A man can easily become jealous of the additional attention his wife gives to the baby. He is jealous, because he feels pulled by both sides of this new emotional triangle. As much as each parent may want the other to love the baby, they cannot always control their own needs and jealousies.

On the other side of the picture are those women who are so eager for their husbands to be an equal partner in the triangle that they force too much bonding on them. "I was so eager for my daughter to know her father as well as she knew me and for them to have the identical emotional bond that she and I have that I would practically force her on him every evening," said Ina. "He would come home after an hour commute and I would expect him to be eager to spend an hour playing with her before dinner. He loves her and is very attached, but he wasn't always ready for the forced playtime. He finally talked to me about it and we worked it out so that we're both happy with it."

Whatever their philosophies of father-child relations, most women find they feel torn by the emotional and physical demands pulling them in two directions. They are usually the primary emotional and physical support of the child, and yet they are expected to continue to be a full-time helpmate and lover to their husbands. It is not an easy adjustment. Even women who expressed resentment over their husbands' fascination with the child felt torn themselves by the dual demands.

Added to the emotional demands was the real issue of who was to be the physical caretaker of the child. Some women feel it is their job, and if their husbands want to take part in dressing or diaper changing they feel that they are being told they are inadequate or that they are being elbowed out of their rightful place because his love for the child is greater than his love for her.

Other women await their husbands' return from work so they can share some of the baby care, because they feel smothered by motherly duties. If the husband feels that is "women's work" and won't participate, the wife may feel isolated and unloved or wonder if her husband really loves the child.

There are many couples, especially in families where both mother and father work, who may have problems with the physical caretaking. The emotional and caretaker roles may be divided up with little problem. It should be remembered by both, however, that when father is taking care of the children he is not "babysitting," he is parenting in the same sense as the mother. Most women who work outside the home find that they are still stuck with a major portion of domestic responsibilities. Families who manage to achieve a 50-50 split on chores are rare. Being a giving, self-sacrificing parent is expected of a woman; rarely are mothers complimented on the job they do, no matter how hard they work to fulfull their parental responsibilities. On the other hand, men who handle a minimal amount of diapering, bathing, and feeding chores can almost always count on being told by friends and relatives that they are wonderful fathers.

"With three children I have to work," explained Dorian. "I work as a nurse three nights a week and on weekends. It was really hard for me at first. I wasn't comfortable leaving the care of the children to my husband, because women are supposed to be so much better at it. I felt as if any incident was my fault for going away. But now I've realized that he can handle it as well as I can. So he does things a little differently than I, what does that mean? It hasn't hurt the children."

However, arriving at a balance and forming each one's own role in the new three-member family group is probably the most difficult set of adjustments that must be faced by every set of new parents, no matter what their preconceived feelings about the roles of mother and father or how they imagined parenthood would strike them emotionally. The realization that one is now sharing the love and time of the one person who was "theirs" and that one must also begin to divide up one's self between two people can be a very trying adjustment for the couple. Somehow an equilibrium must be found.

## The Baby Is the Center of Their Lives

Quite naturally, the baby immediately becomes the center of its parents' lives. Why shouldn't it? Everything they are now doing, from feedings and loss of sleep to the emotional and physical energies pulling at them, focus around the baby.

The baby is probably even the literal centerpiece at the table as they eat dinner each evening. More than half of the women interviewed described eating dinner with the baby propped up in an infant seat sitting in the middle of the table. They had varied reactions to this new addition to their dining rooms.

"I hated it," said Amanda. "I remember calling my mother crying hysterically one evening because I was convinced we were never going to get to eat ever again without having the baby there."

But Celia remembers her situation differently. "We enjoyed it. It was really very easy. He kept quiet because he felt part of what we were doing, and we got to enjoy watching him and having a quiet, unhurried meal together, too."

A woman may be sensitive to the new role of the baby as the central element in her life, particularly if she has watched the child all day. By the time her husband comes home, she is dying for adult companionship and an intelligent conversation. But he has not observed the baby's every reaction all day, so usually he wants to spend the first minutes home talking about the baby.

Some women described how going out to dinner became a disaster for them. They would eagerly look forward to being away from the baby and having an opportunity to talk about something else, or even just a quiet, romantic, candlelit meal, and instead would find themselves playing "20 questions" while the new fathers got caught up on every detail of the child's growth during the week. By the time dinner was over, the women were furious at their husbands.

Of course, communication is the key here once again. If a woman doesn't want to talk about the baby, but wants an evening of complete diversion, she should tell her husband. Professional counselors report that most men, if forewarned, will consciously avoid even mentioning the child all evening. They also report that within an hour or so, ninety-nine out of one hundred women will bring up the baby themselves and use the evening out as a nice, quiet time to discuss issues related to the baby. After all, the baby *is* the center of their lives.

# Sharing Needs

Since the baby has added so many new elements to their lives, both parents also have new needs that they begin to expect the other to anticipate and help to ease.

The need mentioned most often by women is to be away from the baby once in a while. Women with a mother, sister, or other female relative in their immediate area were able to solve this problem by leaving the child with the relative for a few hours once a week and just getting out to shop or have lunch with a friend. Those who were not so lucky all described coping as long as they could before they requested an arrangement with their husbands. For most, six or seven months of constant baby care were the limit. After that their own personal needs took a priority.

Some women find it possible to hook up with another new mother and they either take turns relieving one another for daytime babysitting or they hire a sitter to care for both their children, possibly one day a week on a regular basis. If an arrangement of this kind continues, the children become friends and learn to socialize at an early age. If the mothers are supportive, not competitive, they can be very helpful to one another—evaluating the sitter, sharing ideas and concerns.

Most women were able to convince their husbands to give them vacation time. Leslie and her husband, a doctor, agreed that he would watch the twins all afternoon on his weekday off. Geraldine and her husband agreed that he would take full charge of the baby in the evenings when she wanted to go out to a club meeting or some other activity. Cassie and Ian designated one night each week when they would always get a sitter and go out. Many of the couples made arrangements that not only satisfied the women, but were pleasing to the men, too. Many of the new fathers, it seems, wanted a chance to be alone with their children without their wives constantly looking over their shoulders and supervising their play.

"Luke is a bigger baby than the kids," laughed Holly. "When I can't stand being with the kids any more I tell him to take charge and I disappear . . . sometimes just to our room to read. Inevitably, he gets too rough and hurts himself. Twice I've had to send him to the hospital for stitches!"

"Harold loves it when I go out and he can give her a bath, play with her, and spoil her," said Geraldine. "But I never know what I'm coming home to. Once when she was first walking, she shut the bathroom door and the latch slipped, locking him out. By the time I got home she was sleeping like an angel, but he was still hyper-ventilating from panicking and kicking down the door to get to her."

Allowing each other to have time with and without the child can help to make both the parent-child and wife-husband relationships stronger. Many of the women also commented that they had been so fatigued and uncertain of their own abilities to do things, that they had needed their husbands' reassurance and help to even do the mandatory entertaining of relatives and friends eager to see the new arrival. If the husbands would participate in the planning, even on a basic level such as taking over all beverages or selecting menu items, it not only helped the women, but it made the men feel like a necessary part of the process.

"I remember Joe and I worked on all the details of the christening and the party for twenty-five or thirty relatives together. It was the first thing we had done together in a long, long, time," said Ruth. "It brought us together as a couple again."

Several women mentioned problems the first day they brought the baby home. They described their uncertainty as to what to do. The seemingly routine tasks, which would soon become second nature but were still very new, were the hardest for them to handle. Things like preparing bottles, folding a cloth diaper, or deciding whether to give a supplementary bottle if the baby continued to cry after having a full nursing. Often sharing the decision helps to ease the pressure and ensure that the father is an active partner in the parenting process.

Sharing and helping each other fill basic needs are vital to the health of the individuals and the husband-wife relationship during the early months of parenthood. Sharing brings the couple together and takes some of the demand off the mother, who has so much to do in terms of both emotional and physical baby care. Even if it is only doing the laundry, shopping, or sterilizing bottles in the evening, the husband's efforts to lighten the load and help fill some of her basic needs (and probably his own need to be an insider in this new family) can work wonders to reduce the drudgery of the post partum and make a woman feel more like herself sooner.

# Lifestyle Changes

One month ago the couple worked days and played nights. They went out in the evenings to friends' homes, to movies, for dinner. Suddenly, they are housebound. They have a new infant who must be fed, diapered, and burped every few hours. They spend most of the evening playing with the baby and staring at each other like zombies. Even if they weren't too tired to go out, they can't afford to because diapers, pediatricians, baby clothes, and baby furniture are expensive and they probably no longer have the woman's income.

"It was especially difficult for Larry, although I felt it, too," said Karen. "We had been used to going out almost every night and going away for weekends with almost no notice, and that was gone. Larry went on an 'I'm losing my youth' kick. He decided he was missing out on life. It was a big adjustment for him."

Heather agreed. "We used to go out a lot, drink a lot and stay out to all hours," she explained. "Now we rarely stay out late, we hardly drink, and we tend to have people over for a quiet evening at home rather than go to big group events or parties. Frankly, I think it's a positive change for us."

"We definitely go out less," said Leslie. "The main reason is the cost. A few weeks ago we went out for pizza and a movie. By the time we paid for the babysitter, the food, and the show it was over forty dollars. That's a big blow to the budget."

Many couples reported slowly losing contact with childless friends after the baby arrived, another lifestyle change that was difficult for them to accept. For many women this is a serious problem as they watch a very close friend, in whom they confided and relied, slowly drifting away because of the differences in interests and the new mother's lack of freedom to go out as often as she once did.

"It becomes really difficult to get together with people without kids after you have a baby," explained Leslie. "We just don't have that much to say besides talking about the kids, and they're not that interested. We miss their company, but that just seems to be the way life is right now."

Geraldine told of having lost a very close friend who could not cope with her own jealousy of Geraldine's new child. The friend could not have children of her own. "Losing contact with someone with whom you have been close is very painful, and it makes the adjustment to parenthood that much more difficult because you cannot share your happy moments with that friend, but it was obvious right from the day my daughter was born that this friend would not be able to come to terms with her own loneliness and we drifted apart quickly."

Another change that is felt immediately by the couple is the loss of work-free weekends. Before the baby came, weekends were special, something to look forward to. After baby, weekend days become the same as the rest of the week. Gone are sleeping late and spontaneously deciding to go somewhere just for fun or to stay in bed and make love all day. The baby will wake up at its regular feeding time whether it is Saturday or Tuesday and so will the parent, probably the mother, who is responsible for the morning care of the child.

Going anywhere requires planning and preparation. A bag of diapers, clothes, and other necessities must be packed even to go shopping for the afternoon. Babysitters usually cannot be found at the last minute, so impromptu movies or dinners out with friends are out of the question.

In addition, by six or eight weeks, the woman and the baby have probably developed some kind of sleeping and eating routine during the week to which they are adjusted. Daddy, on the other hand, is oblivious to this. He may decide he wants to go somewhere just as it is time for baby to nap or be fed. While routines must be kept flexible, if it is time for the baby's two o'clock feeding, it's better to do it at home than in the moving car. The husband may scoot out to do his errands rather than wait the half hour or longer (if the child is nursing) the feeding will take. The woman, who may have been waiting all week for a chance to go out as a family, will end up sitting at home, angry. On the other hand, if she goes and feeds the child en route or at the store, she may find she spends her whole afternoon soothing an irritated baby and might as well have sat home. Some flexibility with a baby's schedule is essential. It is very difficult to plan time away from home with an infant, but it is certainly possible. Babies can adapt to change if it is handled with forethought and planning.

# Learning to Love Clutter

Newborn babies are so tiny, they'll fit in a large hat box if necessary. Yet within days after the birth, the house or apartment they have entered looks like a warehouse.

Babies come with equipment and toys. The average baby from a middle-income family has a crib, changing table, playpen, highchair, infant seat, and possibly an indoor swing (which allegedly keeps baby dozing during meals and allows for peaceful digestion by the parents). There may also be a dresser and probably at least half a dozen stuffed animals that always seem to move around the house of their own volition.

More than a few new mothers have been heard screaming that they can no longer stand living amid the chaos. And even more new fathers cannot understand why the house looks like a mess all the time when "all the woman does is take care of the baby." The place may not be a mess at all, just crowded by baby's possessions. If your space is limited, buy baby equipment only when the need becomes apparent. Changing tables, coach carriages, swings, and playpens are not used by all parents. Buy only necessary items to avoid clutter.

Finding the time to keep the house clean is hard enough for a new mother, but the added hardware and goodies that have eaten up valuable floor space make it seem even worse. The place always looks cluttered and crowded no matter how hard she cleans.

"I felt inadequate," said Holly. "I couldn't keep the house looking clean. I thought about a cleaning woman, but that really wouldn't have helped. I finally made a rule—no toys or other children's things would go into the livingroom. That helped. Fortunately summer came and I could take the kids to play outside, too. That saved me. It probably saved a lot of hassle between us, too. I didn't feel as tired and penned in, and I could deal with everything better. When that stuff is all over the house you start to feel crazy."

# Illness

Any congenital birth defect in the child can be especially traumatic for the couple. They may feel guilty or inadequate for having created an imperfect child and upset by the pain the child must suffer.

Monica's son had an enlarged hydrocele (fluid in the scrotum). Such a problem is not uncommon in newborn boys, but it may require surgery. In this case surgery was required when the baby was four months old.

"I remember I watched the enlargement constantly. It was so disproportionate. I worried a lot," she recalled. "When you take a child that small for surgery it's very hard. That's all you can think about for weeks. During the week he was hospitalized I was there from the minute he woke up in the morning until he fell asleep at night. It was very depressing for my husband and me. So many things go through your mind. I think that's when we understood what parenthood was. We really grew up fast."

Mona's daughter had a congenital dislocated left hip, a correctible problem but one that is distressing and very hard to face for new parents. "When I was first told, I think I was in shock," she remembered. "It was very difficult to face. When we took her home from the hospital a harness was strapped across her chest and all the way down both legs. It was very traumatic seeing this six-pound baby with this huge strap and her legs spread out. My mother-in-law couldn't stop crying when she saw her, and I cried most of the way home. She was in that harness for three months.

"The harness made life more difficult. I couldn't use cloth diapers and had to go to the more expensive disposables. Caring for her took more adjustment and learning to manage with the harness. We both had a lot of difficulty adjusting to our new lifestyle, and I'm sure the hip problem added to it."

Today Mona's daughter is fine—she even goes to ballet class and toddler gymnastics—but during those first months her condition increased her parents' difficulties in working together to become a family and added to Mona's feelings of isolation.

Holly's youngest daughter was born with an ugly, black birthmark on her leg. The pediatrician felt it would have to surgically removed as soon as the child was old enough, or it was sure to become malignant during puberty. "I became depressed," remembers Holly. "I spent one day in the hospital just crying. I suppose it could have been called the 'blues,' but it was more than that. I didn't have a perfect baby. That really bothered me. It still bothers me, even though I have decided by now to count my blessings—at least it can be removed. But this baby was the only one of my children with whom I had any depression afterward, and I'm sure it was because of the birthmark. I took her to three doctors for opinions."

The depression served to add to Holly's feelings of fatigue, making it more difficult for her to bounce back as mother and sexual partner.

Any illness in the child can affect the couple's readjustment to each other as well as their adjustment to parenthood. Experts say even the chance of illness or a phobia one of the parents may have can become overwhelming when combined with the emotional stress of new parenthood and the bond to the infant.

# Every Child Is Beautiful

Of course, not all babies are born beautiful, or even cute. Some babies are born with marks all over their skin, puffy faces from the trauma of birth, ugly, deformed-looking heads because of the pressure from vaginal delivery, or a myriad of other imperfections. All of these will go away in a few days or weeks, but it can be very upsetting, especially for the mother, to discover that her progeny is what pediatricians call an "F.L.K." (a funny-looking kid). It is a blow to the parents' egos to have the ugliest baby in the nursery and may cause even a secure woman to question her own physical beauty. If she were truly attractive could she create this child? Having an F.L.K. can add to the "blues" and slow down the development of mother-child love and the normal acceptance of the new parental role.

"When my first was born I was very young and quite insecure," explained Catsy. "His head became very misshapen in the delivery, and he had a lazy eyelid that didn't quite open all the way. I went down to the nursery to look at him the second day, and there were two women looking at the babies. One pointed to him and said 'Isn't that the ugliest baby you've ever seen?' I was devastated. I ran back to my room crying. It took me a long time to accept the fact that I was his mother and to really love him. I know I loved my second child much more easily because he was really a beautiful baby."

Nancy's daughter was so badly bruised in the delivery process that her face was swollen and discolored at birth. "She was definitely one of the ugliest babies I've ever seen, but she was very alert, so I tried to ignore it as best I could, but it was difficult to accept that my child was ugly. It was kind of embarrassing. However, my second was born by Caesarean and he was absolutely perfect-looking and gorgeous. The nurse asked me if they could use him as the model baby for the class on how to bathe an infant. I was so proud. You cannot imagine what it meant to me to have such a beautiful child after my first experience. It was like a great victory."

# Economics

"One of the biggest adjustments we had to make was monetary," explained Jenny. "Since I'm not working, we've cut our income in half. It was a conscious decision we made, but the limits of our budget have become a big issue. Intellectually we knew there would be a difference, but it is hard to come to grips with this on a day-to-day basis. It's difficult not to have money for something you might have bought without thinking about a few months before."

In fact, in families where both parents worked before the baby and the woman does not return to work afterward, money can become the biggest single cause of arguments and interpersonal anxiety. When the child comes and the wife does not return to work, an imbalance occurs. Family consumption increases, while income declines. Besides normal costs of food, heat, rent (or mortgage), clothing and gasoline, babies are expensive. Studies have shown that new parents spend considerably more on detergents, soap powders, baby foods, cereals, vitamins, cough medicine and other cold remedies than the general population, and items such as disposable diapers, baby powders and ointment weren't even added to the totals. In addition, new parents are pushovers for dolls, wagons, sleds, and other childhood favorites.

The man may feel responsible to earn more money and think that budget problems are a negative reflection on him as a breadwinner. The result can easily be family arguments and feelings of guilt on both sides.

"I went through a rough time when I felt guilty about not bringing home a paycheck," said Anna. "I blamed him for my guilt, because he would show me the bills and say this wasn't his fault, it wouldn't be a problem if I was still working. That hurt me. Of course, it was his way of coping, too. It was easier if he could put the burden on someone else's shoulders. I would get upset and take the guilt.

"One day we both got so upset we had to talk and thrash it out. I told him I was not guilty. I work hard at home as the mother of our child. I keep the house clean. I do virtually everything for him and the baby, and that's hard work. He agreed, and I stopped carrying the guilt."

What Anna described happens in many families. Economic pressure can become very divisive. It is something that must be talked out and settled before either or both adults start to seethe with animosity because of the guilt and budgetary limitations caused by the economic crunch.

Most couples find that their former budgets and priorities in household spending must be changed to accommodate new financial needs created by the baby. They need to discuss their buying habits and needs and decide where they can economize, where they can't, and how they can best use their available funds. Depending on whether the child is bottle- or breast-fed, or wearing disposable or cloth diapers, the added expense to the family budget of the newborn may be as much as $30 or more each week just for necessities. Many couples take loans to purchase the crib and other bedroom furniture the child requires, adding more to monthly bills. Even if the mother goes back to work when the child is a few months old, she may find that child care eats up more than half of her weekly paycheck, still leaving them with a budgetary imbalance.

Most couples find they must make choices, which are not always easy. They must assess their values. What can they comfortably give up? What do they consider luxuries? They may find they will stay home on Saturday nights more, eat less beef and more chicken. Many women said they sat down and listed every item they spent money on during a week in order of priority. Those items that came out at the bottom of the list were either eliminated or purchased less frequently. Not only were these difficult decisions, but they were often very disturbing to one or the other of the couple because the elimination or reduction of some items changed established patterns they had come to expect and enjoy (regular movie nights, wine with dinner, and the like).

"We also finally admitted that we weren't going to be able to save money," added Anna. "That was difficult for me to accept, because I am not happy with having to raise our son in the rough neighborhood in which we now live. But I had to accept it. It will be ten years or more before we can save the down payment for even a small house. My husband is an electrician who works all the overtime he can get, but we have had to reduce our hopes and plans considerably since the baby came."

Connie explained: "It's the shock of suddenly having to account for every dollar and wondering whether you can afford to live the way you had planned that causes problems. Tensions build every time there are bills to pay. You end up arguing, and then you both feel guilty afterwards. It's not real nourishing for a relationship, that's for sure."

# Even Parents Have Parents

Another aspect of new parenthood is that it gives the parents an entirely different perspective on their own parents and why they may have done many of the things they did while the children were growing up. For their parents it also causes a change in the relationship. Suddenly they look upon their children as adults and treat them differently, another change the couple must face.

The couple suddenly find themselves on a peer level with their parents. They realize what their parents went through, the kind of choices and decisions they had to make, and often their parents' opinions suddenly carry more weight. A new level of mutual respect can often result.

Women may turn to their mothers, rather than their husbands, if questions arise about the child. A man may be hurt when he sees his wife taking counsel from her mother on feeding or clothing the child instead of making these decisions as a couple. Today, when many men take an active part in child rearing, this can become an issue between the couple.

Interestingly, researchers have found that the way a woman perceives her mother will have a direct effect on what kind of a mother she herself will be. Studies have shown that if a woman has a good relationship with her mother she will be a warmer, more affectionate parent herself. Similarly, a man's perception of his father will affect the kind of father he becomes, although probably to a lesser degree in today's world. How many fathers in past generations participated in the birth process compared with the number that enter the delivery room with their wives today?

Most of the problems that may arise between the couple during the post partum year can be solved by the couple themselves through communication, compromise, and working hard to correct the situation. Being a parent requires work, decisions, choices, and often giving up things one previously valued, in the interest of the child or the marriage. As each individual struggles to grow and adapt, the relationship as a couple may be strained, but with a conscious effort by each of them it will stretch, not break.

## CHAPTER SIX
# **Sexuality**

*"All of us who had babies around the same time would joke about our sex lives a lot. We'd say we should tell our husbands that the doctor said we can't do it . . . but that wouldn't work. The doctors never say 'can't',"* laughed Monica.

*"It was at least three months after the baby's birth before we had sex again. I don't think I was fit to talk to let alone make love with before then,"* Laura reported.

Probably the biggest single issue after the birth of a child is the reestablishment of a sex life for the couple. Many women are surprised and bewildered by the fact that, in most cases, there is not a fairly automatic return to prepregnancy sexuality. Even many second-timers, who may not have had a problem after the first, can find they have no sex drive at all after the second child. All of these women are unprepared to deal with this unexpected crisis.

These women vary in adaptability, often developing deep-seated fears of inadequacy, of physical or emotional defects in themselves.

In our society a woman is expected to be all things—wife, mother, housekeeper, perhaps working woman, and an eager lover. Thus, after the birth of a child, guilt about not fulfilling her husband's physical needs can become overwhelming, especially if he does not respond sympathetically to her feelings.

Nursing mothers can have additional problems stemming from the hormonal levels needed to lactate, added fatigue, and the inconvenience of sometimes sensitive, leaking breasts.

Most obstetricians advise their patients not to resume sexual intercourse for six weeks after the birth as a precaution against possible infection. More recently, a small number of doctors, in response to articles in medical journals which claim six weeks is too long for many couples, have begun to reduce that restriction to four or even three weeks. Every woman should listen to her own doctor and not resume sexual intercourse until he/she gives the go-ahead. Any woman who feels she does not want to wait six weeks should ask for an earlier appointment with her doctor.

# Part I: The First Six Weeks

## Pain Can Be Real

There is no question that many women may experience very real pain as a residual effect of childbirth.

The most common is pain from the episiotomy and the subsequent scar. This is probably at its worst during the first few days after birth, but, depending on the woman's own natural healing ability or tendency toward scarring, may be a problem for weeks.  ·

Some women, however, also find that the episiotomy has the residual effect of improving their sex lives in the long run. Because the episiotomy reduces the stretching of the vagina and perineum, it can actually help to preserve vaginal elasticity and strength and prevent possible prolapse of the uterus or stress incontinence (inability to control urination when coughing, sneezing, etc.).

Valerie experienced so much pain from the episiotomy, she began to wish she had had a Caesarean. "I remember watching the Caesarean mothers in the hospital wandering all over with no difficulty, while I was in such pain I could barely put one foot in front of the other," she recalled.

In a survey done in Utah, twenty-three of forty-two women complained of continuing, annoying pain from the episiotomy which still hindered the resumption of sex six weeks or more after the birth.

Ina reported having a burning sensation in the area of the episiotomy for many weeks after the birth of her first child. Small lumps formed on one side of Erica's episiotomy scar after her second child was delivered. The lumps appear to be permanent and have required the couple to make adjustments during sexual intercourse for comfort.

As certainly as every woman is an individual with an individual body chemistry, every woman will heal differently. While most women describe only moderate discomfort for a few days, some do experience great pain or long-term effects from the episiotomy.

Healing of the episiotomy can be promoted by remembering to follow the recommended cleansing and care procedures that will be suggested in childbirth classes, by the doctor, or by the nurses in the hospital. These include:

- Bathe regularly with warm water and mild soap to maintain cleanliness.
- Use dry heat, such as a heat lamp, directly on the area three times a day to help dry the incision and promote healing.
- If regular care and heat treatments do not relieve the problem, consult a doctor for an analgesic spray or ointment.

Babies are larger today than they were in the last generation due to better nutrition and improved prenatal care, so even with the episiotomy some women may tear the rectum or vaginal wall, or require a larger incision during delivery. Such women can expect a longer period of discomfort and should not be embarrassed to speak to the doctor or hospital nurses about receiving a mild pain reliever.

Hemorrhoids (varicose veins in the rectal area) can be another new-found source of pain after birth. Fully one-third of the women studied developed hemorroids during the immediate post partum period. With several of the women, the hemorrhoids appeared almost immediately after the birth, a result of lengthy pushing in the delivery room. The rest appeared within a few weeks, often bleeding frequently when first developing, creating fear of cancer or some other dread disease before being diagnosed in a visit to the doctor. When hemorrhoids flare up, the last thing a woman wants to think about is sexual intercourse.

Caesarean mothers may expect the discomfort of the stitches and scar, which will probably ache or burn for ten days to two weeks. The pain often changes to numbness during the first six weeks, which may persist for several months. In addition, Caesarean mothers can expect pain during the first eight days from gas. Gas in the bowel is the natural result of surgery because of the interruption in the natural flow of food which follows the procedure. The gas that collects is similar to a baby's colic. Many women find the pain from the gas worse than that from the stitches.

"I remember my husband came in with cakes and baby gifts and wanted me to share this exciting emotional experience with him, and all I wanted to do was lie there and do my Lamaze breathing to try to handle the terrible cramps I had," remembers Geraldine. "Instead of getting hand holding and cuddling, he got chased out. I just wanted to be alone."

# Fatigue

Fatigue has already been discussed (see chapter 4) as an ever-present, seemingly never-ending problem of the first year post partum. It has an enormous effect on the sexuality of the woman during that time.

Many women described being so totally exhausted during the first six weeks that they really couldn't care less what their husbands were feeling, nor did they have any interest in any physical contact with their husbands.

"All I wanted to do was sleep," explained Donna. "I was totally exhausted and didn't even have the energy or interest to talk to him, never mind thinking about cuddling or satisfying his sexual needs in some way."

Nursing mothers can expect to be even more tired because they are using more of their body energy to produce the food needed to nurture the baby.

# Renewed Sexual Contact

Most couples have abstained from sexual intercourse at the recommendation of the obstetrician for the last four to six weeks of pregnancy. Now the baby is here and they must abstain for six more weeks. For many couples, this abstinance is extremely difficult.

In all probability, the husband is much more eager for a return to sexual intimacy than his wife. Most women find they have never felt less sexy in their lives than they do during the first few weeks post partum. They describe being very tired, covered with ugly stretch marks, and very aware of the excess weight they are still carrying. Yet it is essential that both of them, man and woman, make some effort to renew their sexual contact as soon as possible.

*Sexual intercourse* is generally prohibited by the doctor for six weeks to permit the stitches and the uterine lining to heal safely, without the introduction of new bacteria that might enter with intercourse. However, *sex* is not prohibited. There are many things a couple can do to begin to revive that closeness before the six-week checkup.

"I remember the first few weeks after going home from the hospital, I felt extremely close to my husband. I couldn't quite believe we had a child, that I was a mother and he was a father. I really wanted to cuddle up to him. We were very intimate without having intercourse," according to Brooke.

Virtually anything goes except sexual intercourse. The couple may cuddle, snuggle, hug and kiss all they want. The use of external vibrators, even for the woman to reach orgasm is not prohibited. In fact, it is suggested and recommended by many doctors and sex therapists, so long as the vibrator is not inserted into the vagina where it might cause infection. There is also no reason why the woman cannot reduce her guilt feelings over not being able to have intercourse by giving her husband sexual satisfaction through manual manipulation or oral-genital sex.

Some women have found that telling their husbands that it is okay for them to masturbate worked for their relationship, however, expert counselors suggest that women exercise care in using this alternative. If approval of the husband's masturbation was never discussed prior to the birth of the infant, the husband may take the suggestion as a rejection, coming as it does while the wife is so deeply involved with the child.

One woman with a particularly open relationship with her husband reported that masturbation did ease their sexual problems: "Besides the six-week rule, I was in a lot of pain. Even my six-week checkup was painful. My husband was very eager for sex. I'm not shy, so I told him I'd be perfectly happy if he masturbated. He's not shy either, so he did. For us, it was a good temporary solution."

# Female Masturbation

A woman who was in the habit of regular masturbation prior to her delivery may feel ready to begin masturbating again before the six-week checkup. It is always wise to ask the doctor whether one is sufficiently healed to masturbate safely, but generally if she masturbates through clitoral stimulus and does not have any stitches between the vagina and clitoris there is probably no reason she cannot resume her regular pattern of masturbation as soon as she feels ready.

However, a woman who habitually masturbates through vaginal stimulus should not resume masturbation until after she has been cleared by her doctor at the six-week checkup. The restriction is similar to that against sexual intercourse. No foreign object that may carry bacteria should enter the vagina until healing is complete in order to prevent infection.

# Breaking the Six-Week Rule

Almost one-quarter of the women interviewed admitted sheepishly to having violated the six-week prohibition against sexual intercourse. Half of them said they had wanted to have intercourse because of their own drives, the rest explained that they had merely done their "wifely duty."

About one-quarter of the violators said sexual intercourse actually felt better after the baby was born than before, but only a few of those women had strong enough sex drives to want to have intercourse at the same frequency they had prior to the birth.

Of the women who said they had returned to sexual intercourse before the six-week checkup to please their mates, only a third said they had enjoyed sex and quickly found it to be as satisfying as it had been before.

The comments expressed by the others varied from not feeling comfortable because of the episiotomy, to not feeling comfortable because of leaking breasts, not having a true sex drive, the experience being too mechanical, and sex just not being enjoyable.

Couples who had difficulty or discomfort with sex during the early weeks often blamed the way the doctor had stitched the episiotomy. Doctors have found that often the husbands will ask them to sew the episiotomy "loose" or "tight." Even though it is embarrassing for the woman, the doctor may play along jokingly in an attempt to distract the woman while she is being sewed. Many couples firmly believe that if sex is uncomfortable, especially during the early weeks or months, it is because the doctor made the episiotomy too tight. Several couples reported having nasty arguments after attempting intercourse, during which the wife would blame the husband, saying the discomfort was his fault because he had requested a "tight" episiotomy.

In fact, the doctor does not control the tightness or looseness of the perineum or the vagina through the episiotomy. All episiotomies are repaired by just putting the tissue back together. No matter what the husband answers, the doctor does not take a tuck or a dart in the perineum, he merely joins the two edges created by the episiotomy incision together. Tightness or looseness depends on how well the woman heals.

# Nature's Contraception

Many women are very upset to discover that their sex drive is severely diminished after childbirth. They expect to be so exhilarated and emotional that sex will be a must. Instead they are tired, perhaps sore, and so absorbed with the baby they don't think of sex at all.

However, since in Western society there are no harems, a woman is expected to supply all of her man's needs on her own—including sexual needs. Whether one agrees or disagrees with our culture, it dictates that a man has appetites and his woman must feed those appetites. A better attitude for all couples would be one of maturity, sensitivity, and understanding, but society hasn't reached that level yet.

Thus, when the husband wants regular sexual intercourse and the wife does not, she may begin to worry needlessly that she has a problem. She worries that she may be deficient as a woman and as a lover. Is something wrong that she cannot give equal energy to making love with her husband as she is giving to caring for the child?

Certainly not! The lack of sex drive during the first six weeks is "nature's contraception." It can take the full six weeks and more for hormonal levels to settle down from the changes caused by pregnancy. There may be an annoying and irritating vaginal discharge that is not conducive to sexual intercourse. A woman may be exhausted, have sore, leaking breasts, feel fat, or have some discomfort, and thus not feel terribly sexy. Any one or any combination of these legitimate, physical reactions may be occurring in her body. Every case is individual.

Masters and Johnson interviewed 111 women during the first three months post partum. Forty-seven of the women described having low or negligible interest in sex during that time, 11 women said they had equal or better interest in sex, and 43 described varying responses. Some of them described continuing pain from the episiotomy or vaginal irritation as deterrents to frequent sexual intercourse (*Human Sexual Response*).

Nature itself seems to have a few methods of giving the body time to heal before encouraging it to become pregnant again. A woman who is not eager for sexual intercourse because of signals she is receiving from her own body should not be worrying about her femininity. Nature's message is "if it doesn't feel good, you won't do it."

# Part II: The Later Months, Or, Things Don't Change Overnight

## But It Hurts

A woman goes for her six-week checkup believing that, magically, once the doctor gives his seal of approval she is completely healed and back to normal.

That night, her husband puts champagne on ice. They are going to have wonderful, passionate sex, or so they think. They consume the entire bottle, slip into bed, passion grows. Finally, he enters her. Instead of sighing with rapture, she screams, "Get out, your penis feels like a knife!"

In fact, for many couples, the first night of sexual renewal after the birth of their child will become the beginning of an issue in their relationship that must be solved. Instead of marking the end of a long period of abstinence and the return to a normal sexual life, the first attempt at love-making after the six-week checkup in many cases signals the start of a problem that may last for many months.

Even the women (about 10 percent) who said they found sexual intercourse as good or better than before the baby was born admitted to opting to make love less frequently than in the past because they were simply too tired.

One new mother explained: "Sex actually felt better after the birth, but we still did it less frequently than we would have liked. I was always just pooped by evening. It took a while before we realized we had to wake up early in the morning to mess around before the kids got up. Then we'd both be awake and enjoy it."

Many couples find they both feel guilty and frustrated by their inability to overcome the physical and emotional factors that may hamper their physical relationship. These "distractors" come in many forms.

# The Physical "Distractors"

The most universal physical problem which even the most relaxed and satisfied new mother will experience is fatigue. The physical exhaustion that is a natural part of raising a new baby for at least the first three months (see chapter 4) also takes its toll on the couple's sex life.

"I remember looking at the clock and thinking 'Well, it's 10:30, I just got her down to sleep. She'll be up at 2 A.M. He'll come to bed at 11:30. If he wants to make love, that will take until 12:30. Is it worth that time? I could be sleeping for those hours," remembered Amanda.

Because of the fatigue problem, the couple must deal with an immediate loss of spontaneity. They must plan sexual encounters in advance, to adjust to each other's needs.

Kimberly described going for counseling because her husband was angry because they rarely made love after the baby was born. "He likes to watch the eleven o'clock news, and I would fall asleep and not be eagerly waiting for him at 11:30. By nine o'clock I was usually ready for bed. The counselor told him get into bed with me at nine, make love, and then, after I fell asleep, go watch the news. Nobody ordained that you must fall asleep immediately after sex."

Fatigue is a real physical problem, not an illusion. Unfortunately, no matter how much the wife may want to make love, if she is really exhausted the fatigue will win and she will fall asleep. Then they will both be furious the next day because another opportunity to make love was missed. This will happen again and again unless they can learn to adjust to this new "distractor" in their lives.

Virtually all of the women interviewed for this study said sex was a problem in the evenings for at least three to five months because of the fatigue. Some felt fatigue was still a problem more than a year later, because they were chasing active toddlers around all day by then. They were usually much more interested in sex during the day because they weren't exhausted yet.

Women whose husbands could not be home during the day found the solution to the problem to be carefully scheduling one evening a week in which the baby was put to bed early or shipped off to relatives. Then the couple would settle down for a romantic, candlelit dinner with wine, followed, of course, by sex. Other possible solutions will be discussed later in this chapter.

The second most common physical "distractor" that can affect the sexuality of the couple is pain during intercourse. Almost 90 percent of the women interviewed complained of some discomfort during intercourse for weeks after the six-week checkup. Many said they had experienced severe, even excruciating pain.

Several of these women said they and their husband believed the pain was psychological because they were too engrossed with the baby. While that might be true in a small minority of cases, there are a number of very real physical causes that may result in pain during intercourse for new mothers.

The most obvious cause is residual pain from the episiotomy scar. In some women, the scar may remain tender to the touch for several months.

Obstetrical damage that occurred during childbirth may also be a source of pain for weeks, or even a few months after delivery. Some of these are varicose veins in the labia (lips of the vagina); tears in the blood vessel system of the vagina that may decrease orgasmic response and can, therefore, cause some pain; atrophy of the muscles of the vagina, causing a less sensual response and some pain from the rubbing of the penis against the vaginal wall; slightly thinner vaginal walls, causing a less sensual response and perhaps some tenderness; a neuroma formation that can give exquisite point tenderness in the vagina or perineum, wherever injury occurred.

The woman may have unpleasant smelling vaginal discharge that can cause some irritation, which can be aggravated during intercourse.

Or, her uterus may have dropped to a lower position as a result of pregnancy, and the head of the penis may now be pounding against the cervix during intercourse.

Masters and Johnson found, by testing women at four and eight weeks post partum, that a woman's physical response to sexual stimulation in the vaginal area was considerably slower than prior to pregnancy. The vagina did not become as vasocongested (congestion in the blood vessels is the primary physiological response to sexual stimulation) as it had prepregnancy. As a result, the vagina did not produce natural lubrication the way it had in the past. A lack of natural lubrication, in itself, can be the source of pain, because of the friction that builds up as the dry vaginal walls are rubbed by the penis. It can also hamper entry into the vagina, making the lips seem to be closed because the path is not lubricated and welcoming. This shortage of lubrication may be a fact of life for several months after delivery.

"Love-making was excruciatingly painful for a long time," said Jenny. "I felt as if I wasn't completely healed. I didn't lubricate well and became so irritated that I couldn't even insert and remove my diaphragm without difficulty. After I started using an additional lubricant, it got better. Not terrific, but better. I'd say it was at least seven months before things got back to normal."

Several women described feeling as if their virginity had returned and remembered having loved the cuddling, touching, and other foreplay, but tensing and backing off from intercourse in anticipation of the pain.

All of the possible sources of discomfort during intercourse are normal responses of the body to the post partum period. Hormones are out of balance, going from pregnant to non-pregnant, or to a lactating state, and each woman's body must recover. All of these "distractors" will go away with time, but the promise of the future probably won't help the couple facing the immediate problem.

Not all women experience problems. In fact, a minority of women actually increased their sexual pleasure, or experienced their first true orgasm, during the post partum. The initial increased vascularity of the entire vaginal region after birth may allow those women who had problems with vasocongestion during love-making suddenly to have a much stronger response to sexual stimulation. However, sex researchers have found that those with increased sexual pleasure are definitely not the majority of women.

For the majority who do have problems, sex therapists suggest that removing the goal orientation of sexual contact can help—that is, creating an atmosphere in which intercourse is not the absolute goal of each sexual encounter. The first time sex is resumed after birth, they recommend, should only follow a long, gentle period of time spent in caressing, kissing, and extensive (and intensive) manual and oral stimulation. If the woman can be completely aroused before penetration occurs, the chances are her discomfort, if any, will be minimal.

Too often, once the couple has received the go-ahead from the doctor, they focus on intercourse and skip the foreplay that will help the woman become fully aroused. That foreplay may have been a very special part of their sexual relationship before the baby came, but after a drought of perhaps twelve weeks in sexual intercourse, they are too eager and don't remember to indulge in extensive foreplay. Adequate stimulation plus the use of a lubricant may be the combination that reduces much of the problem rapidly.

A study of 216 post partum women done at Fairfield University in Connecticut showed that roughly two-third of the women preferred being held and cuddled instead of having sexual intercourse for several months after birth. Thus, intensive foreplay was helpful to them.

In addition to the use of extensive foreplay, couples having problems because of pain during intercourse should experiment with different positions. Usually the side-by-side position or the female superior position will allow the woman to control the entrance and depth of penetration of the penis and thus help to alleviate some of the pain.

The side-by-side position is really a misnomer. The couple actually face each other lying on their sides. Intercourse may be achieved by one of several methods, whichever best suits the couple. They may lie face to face in a straight line and he enters her. She may prefer to swing her top leg over him during intercourse. She may put both her legs around him, or she may simply bend one leg at the knee to facilitate entry.

There are two basic forms of the female superior position. In both cases the male lies on his back while the woman sits on top of him. She may prefer one of two angles either leaning forward or sitting up straight. The female superior position is the one which gives the woman most control and often, therefore, the most pleasure. By bending forward or straightening up she can control the depth of penetration and can find the angle that is most pleasing for her.

# Emotional "Distractors"

The addition of the baby into the family creates a triangle that causes emotional crises for both parents, but especially so for the woman. She recognizes almost immediately that she is now responsible for this helpless creature and feels some kind of bond, even if she is not immediately in love with the child.

But she also loves her husband and has strong ties to him, including a physical relationship that requires a strong emotional response from her. In most cases, the husband is ready and eager for sexual intercourse as soon as the doctor gives the okay. His hormones have not been affected, he is not involved with the child all day every day. He thinks everything will be totally back to normal, if not exactly at the six-week mark, then surely within a short time thereafter.

However, almost half of the women studied said they didn't need their husbands sexually for many months after the baby came. They agreed that they were so emotionally drained by the end of the day constantly giving to their children that they had nothing left for their husbands.

"I had no need for sex," said Monica. "I was getting all the loving I needed in the course of the day. I made up excuses. But after a while he was losing patience and I ran out of new ideas for excuses. So I gave in, but the passion was just not there. My loving was used up by bedtime."

"I ran out of excuses" seems to be a cry heard often among new mothers. Even some women who did not experience pain with intercourse often fell back behind the infamous "headache" to avoid having to try to dredge up the emotional strength necessary to make love with their husbands . . . for as long as excuses would work.

Sexual therapists suggest that the women really do need their husbands in an emotional sense, but in a different way from before the child arrived. They need someone to share the emotional drain and support them, say the experts, and if they got that they would feel more sexual.

Besides the emotional drain, many women experienced a clear loss of drive. Some of that loss can be attributed to physical factors such as fatigue, but more often they described it as an emotional rather than physical reaction. Emotional both in cause and effect.

"With my second I was so happy, everything was wonderful," Ruth said. "I had no desire to do anything but hold that baby. I didn't want to be touched. I didn't want to share either myself or the baby with my husband. I was focused on one thing. I apologized to my husband once, but I had absolutely no need for sex at any level whatsoever."

Ruth and her husband dealt with her asexuality and single focus by being patient and waiting for the return of her sexuality and relaxing of the bond to the baby, but many men and women don't cope as well. The women begin to believe they are somehow deficient because they have shut off sexually and are so totally involved with the infant, but they cannot overcome this drive. They develop feelings of inadequacy and extreme guilt. Their feelings are often not helped by their husbands' reactions. Some men respond by nagging and hounding their wives, which increases the woman's feelings of failure.

"I didn't know what was wrong with me," Jackie recalls. "I thought that I had stopped loving my husband. I thought I had real psychological problems, that I must be deeply unhappy to react this way."

Jackie's husband kept nagging her into having sexual intercourse because he believed that doing it more would make her want it again. Instead it made matters worse, because when she found no improvement in her desire or enjoyment, it only served to increase her sense of unworthiness.

Cassie, too, felt totally asexual. She wanted to be a mother and not a wife. When she and her husband did make love, she experienced a great deal of pain from the combination of a large episiotomy scar and her own tenseness. Her doctor suggested she take the birth control pill to adjust her hormones and give her "psychological confidence" because she'd have no fear of becoming pregnant again. She refused the pill because "I didn't want birth control, I didn't want to have sex anymore, period." Cassie and Jackie found that it took them a full year to feel like themselves again sexually, but it did happen gradually.

Fear of physical problems is another form of emotional response.

Some women found that sexual intercourse was uncomfortable for them for many weeks because they anticipated difficulties. They described having had some pain the first time they made love after the birth and then being unable to relax for weeks thereafter. "Everytime we'd start to make love I'd be fine until the time for actual intercourse," said Faith. "Then I'd get so tense, I would tighten up. I'd be anticipating pain and then cause the pain to happen out of my fear. It took a long time, perhaps a couple of months, before I began to relax."

Another common emotional factor inhibiting the rebirth of normal sexuality in some women is the question of how she looks. About a quarter of the women interviewed reported that they really didn't begin to feel sexy again until they began to get their shapes back. For some that was within three or four months: for the less lucky, it took longer.

Besides the need to lose weight, many women complained about having felt ugly because they suddenly grew dark hair on their faces or started to go bald, both hormonal responses to the pregnancy which go away after a few weeks. Others found that the "linea nigra," the dark line that runs from the navel to the pubic hair during pregnancy, did not disappear shortly after delivery as expected. In some cases, the line stayed for months like a disfiguring scar. The line may eventually fade completely or may remain slightly visible for the rest of her life. A few women also found that they would have to learn to live with hairier thighs and belly than they previously had.

Stretch marks were another common complaint. Women who can't stand the sight of the marks on their bodies themselves assume their husbands feel the same way. They rarely ask the husband's opinion, but shy away from physical contact because they don't want to have him see their new ugliness. Most women do not consult their husbands about any of the residual physical marks that may be on their bodies. They believe they are unattractive and ascribe that reaction to their husbands: therefore, they feel unlovable and lacking in sex appeal. A woman who doesn't feel sexy doesn't initiate sexual encounters.

Take any of the possible emotional reactions to the post partum and add the total exhaustion involved in caring for a newborn, and the result will often be a quick temper, or at least a woman who has become overly sensitive and easily irritated by almost anything her husband does.

Many women reported that they found themselves bickering with their husbands over minor issues. They admitted with hindsight that many of the arguments were really rooted in their own lack of self-esteem because of their looks and lack of sexuality during the first post partum months. The majority felt this tendency to be touchy and argumentative continued until they began to feel both sexy and less tired. In some cases that meant as much as ten months or a year after the birth.

# Part III:
# Sex and the Nursing Mother

There is a divergence of opinion in the professional community about the sexuality of nursing mothers. While Masters and Johnson studied twenty-four nursing mothers and found them to be more eager than non-nursing mothers to return to lovemaking and more orgasmic, other reseachers at major universities have found that, in fact, nursing mothers have a more difficult sexual adjustment than non-nursing mothers.

Of the nursing mothers studied for this book, few described themselves as interested in sex or enjoying it. Fully 90 percent described the effect of nursing on their sex lives to be the biggest single surprise and most difficult problem they had to face during the first post partum year. There are both physical and emotional reasons for this apparent lessening of sexuality for many nursing mothers.

## The Physical

In order to nurse, women must have an elevated level of the hormone prolactin, which allows them to lactate. However, high prolactin also causes a decrease in vaginal lubrication. Thus, the nursing mother may find that she does not secrete any natural lubrication when aroused. Without that lubricant, any attempt at intercourse will be most unpleasant.

The women spoke of feeling so dry and closed it was as if there were no vaginal opening at all. They described pain so intense that they could barely walk after having sexual intercourse. This problem lasts much longer than for non-nursing mothers, generally continuing until at least several weeks after the baby is weaned, until the woman's hormonal levels begin to return to normal.

Most doctors recommend a vaginal cream or jelly for lubrication. Some suggest a vaginal estrogen cream to try to artificially replace that hormone, the levels of which have been severely reduced by the hormonal needs caused by nursing.

As long as the new mother's endocrine system remains in a state of hormonal imbalance because of the unusually high levels of prolactin and lowered levels of estrogen, the vaginal area can become sore from any physical contact.

The second physical problem stressed by the women interviewed was once again the great distractor—fatigue. Since most nursing mothers do not have someone bottle-feed the child for the 2 A.M. feeding, they do not get more than two or three hours of sleep at a stretch until the baby sleeps through the night, which may happen early, but probably won't begin for at least eight weeks. The end result is a woman so exhausted she cannot even think about doing anything as draining as making love. All she really wants to do is sleep.

"I was so tired I could barely get up to get the baby," said Nancy. "I remember nursing him alone at 5 A.M. and thinking I didn't have the energy to do this anymore and just crying and crying. When my husband would suggest sex I'd just try to explain that all I wanted to do was sleep."

Tiring as new parenthood is under any circumstances, it appears to be even more so for the nursing mother, unless she is willing to compromise and allow her husband or another person to give the child a bottle for one feeding. Several women recommended that method. After weeks of exhaustion, they began to allow their husbands to give the baby a bottle of either formula or expressed breast milk at 10 P.M. The women could go to bed early in the evening and not awaken until the 2 A.M. feeding. Thus, they would get a full six hours of uninterrupted sleep.

Other physical factors directly affected the ability to make love. Periods of engorgement, when the breasts would be swollen with an oversupply of milk, would be times of pain and leave the woman uninterested in being touched.

Breast soreness, infections, or abscesses resulting from the nursing process had a similar effect. While infections and abscesses require treatment by a physician, breast soreness can be relieved by trying any one of a number of simple home treatments. The first one suggested by all the women was to avoid using any of the so-called breast creams for nursing mothers that can be purchased at the drugstore. All of the women found that the creams kept the nipples too soft. In order to nurse without soreness, the nipples must become tough and calloused.

*The Complete Book of Breastfeeding* and *Nursing Your Baby,* two of the bestselling books about nursing, suggest several steps to reduce breast soreness and more rapidly adjust to nursing which the nursing mothers interviewed felt were excellent. They are:

> a) Keep your nipples dry. This may be accomplished by snipping out the tips of your bras or walking around the house topless and braless whenever possible.
>
> b) Expose your nipples to sunlight or a sunlamp for brief periods during the day, being very careful to avoid sunburn.
>
> c) Use manual expression to start the milk flowing just before the baby is to nurse, so it won't have to suck as hard at first.
>
> d) Nurse for shorter periods of time.
>
> e) Change your position at each feeding so the baby won't always create pressure on the same spots.
>
> f) Ask your doctor for an oxytoxin nasal spray to speed up your letdown reflex.
>
> g) If the nipples are badly cracked, use a nipple shield temporarily.
>
> h) Drink plenty of fluids so you will produce sufficient milk to avoid hard sucking by the baby.

Since many women experienced breast soreness for many weeks during nursing, they found that their sex lives were unexpectedly hampered by their lack of desire to be touched in the affected areas. They reported that using one or more of the suggested treatments did help reduce the pain and let them enjoy being fondled by their husbands again.

Many nursing women seem to become "nipple conscious" while nursing. They examine their nipples regularly and are aware of any little change or variation. Even women who experience little difficulty with nursing watch the progress of callousing and are more aware of every nuance surrounding the nipples. They spoke in particular of a more acute awareness of how their nipples felt during any sexual contact with their husbands. Many complained about a loss of sensitivity to the touch of their nipples, aureolae and breast surfaces which made it more difficult for them to become aroused.

Some women were positive their nipples had lost the ability to become erect on stimulation while they were nursing. Experts believe that the nipples do become erect, but that the aureolae must have enlarged so much that at times it was difficult to perceive the nipples becoming erect. While in some rare cases there may really be a lack of erection, it is probable that in most cases the apparent lack of erection is an optical illusion.

Some women found that their breasts were so enlarged by the nursing that they had to wear their nursing bras to bed to feel comfortable. The bras were not terribly attractive to either the women or their husbands, but they were serving a needed purpose.

One problem that was experienced by virtually every nursing mother was leaking from the breasts. Women generally do not feel terribly sexy when their breasts are leaking and their nightgowns are soaked with breast milk. In addition, many women were surprised to find that their husbands were horrified by the leakage, particularly by the milk women may lose in spurts during sexual activity in response to their arousal.

Many of the men refused to touch their wives' breasts while they were nursing because they were nervous or repulsed at the sight of the milk or the thought that they would be trespassing on the baby's "territory."

One woman thought it might be a sexual turn-on for her if her husband would suck at her breasts like the baby and taste her milk. He was horrified at the thought of violating her sacred mother's milk. Instead of making love, they argued about what she saw as a ridiculous, uninformed attitude, but which he considered to be extremely important. "Even after I gave up trying to get him to taste the milk," she remembered. "Our sex life was still limited because he wouldn't touch me near my breasts. It was mechanical and not much fun."

Men differ in their reactions to nursing and the baby's suckling at the breast. Some may be curious to taste the milk or simply to see what lactating breasts feel like in the mouth. Some may find it repulsive and worry about the effect some bacteria might have on the baby. Neither reaction is unusual or out of the ordinary, and the woman should accept it for what it is. Medically, there is no reason the child's father cannot suck at the breasts as long as the nipples are cleaned before they are next given to the baby; however, the man's feelings should be accepted and he should not be pushed to do something he does not desire.

# The Emotional

In an effort to conquer the physical problems preventing them from enjoying sexual contact while nursing, some women did call their doctors for advice. In a few cases the doctors were very sympathetic and explained the hormonal basis of the problems. However, not all doctors are comfortable with the discussion, so they avoid or make light of the situation. Women who are panicky because they are in agonizing pain during sexual intercourse, or have absolutely no drive and believe they have either a physical or psychological problem, all too frequently call the doctor for help and are answered in a most unsatisfactory manner. Don't accept the "brush-off" from your doctor. Insist on an answer to your problem.

Some doctors try to be humorous and joke "God has ordained you will never enjoy sex again" or a similar cute remark. Others smile pleasantly as they tell the upset patient to "Grin and bear it." Some make a practice of telling women who are experiencing sexual problems six or seven months after the baby was born that they are creating the problem in their own minds because of a fear of pregnancy or anger at their husbands. Nursing is ignored as a possible cause.

Even the organizations dedicated to encouraging nursing and helping nursing mothers tend to play down the associated problems, perhaps in fear that they will dissuade potential nursers.

Of course, some doctors genuinely try to counsel their troubled patients. Some have even become trained in sexual therapy and are well aware of the possible range of problems a couple may face. In fact, the physical problems are very real and are often overpowering to the nursing mother. She may begin to believe that she is somehow defective because she has never heard of anyone else having these problems. Most women are unaware that the vast majority of nursing mothers are to some degree having the very same experience.

Many husbands feel that nursing excludes them from a moment of intimacy. Their anger usually takes the form of pushing for sexual relations for their own reassurance and to assuage their diminished self-esteem. The result for the man is more guilt and probably anger, and the woman feels pressured, inadequate, and cornered.

In some cases, the nursing may compound guilt feelings for the mother. It is physically possible for the baby's sucking to cause sexual arousal in the mother. Although not all nursing mothers find this to be true, some do react to the sucking on their breasts in a sexual way. In occasional cases, the level of eroticism has become so high that it has even produced an orgasmic response.

Many women react to the sexual pleasure they derive from nursing as if it were some bizarre perversion or a sign of a deep-rooted defect in themselves, instead of the involuntary physical response that it is. Their sense of guilt can become so great that they begin to avoid sexual contact with their husbands. In addition, since they have had their sexual needs satisfied via nursing, their desire for intimacy with their husbands decreases.

The nursing mother not only has physical changes working on her body, but different emotions and sexual feelings tearing her into pieces. It is no wonder that many of the nursing mothers interviewed said, "I felt as if my body were not my own while I was nursing."

Because they feel almost alienated from their bodies, many nursing mothers do not feel free to be sexy, as if sex were not right because their bodies were inseparable from the infant. They described feeling a lack of closeness with their spouses, as if the baby were always between them, or with them, in bed.

A few women even felt uncomfortable with the larger breasts that are a necessary by-product of nursing. They felt embarrassed that their measurements were suddenly so monumental. "At first I felt like Dolly Parton or Marilyn Monroe and I liked it," remembered Monica. "But after a while I got tired of having men eye me. I really didn't like it. It didn't feel sexy, just annoying."

## Other Road Blocks

Several women commented that their post partum sexual lives were hampered by external factors.

Ina, for example, had her mother-in-law living with them for six months. While she was a great help with the baby, she was in the bedroom next to Ina's and her husband's. They felt very restricted by her proximity, uncomfortable that she might hear them making love, so they avoided frequent intercourse by mutual consent.

Estelle and Heather both had the baby in their bedroom for five or six months. The baby's presence made them feel self-conscious about making love. Both were positive their sex lives had improved the day the baby was finally moved to its own room.

It seems advisable to avoid both of those situations if at all possible. Why throw more hurdles on the road back to sexual normalcy? Couples need the freedom and comfort to go through the same kind of sexual exploration and adjustment they made with their first sexual experiences. Any physical impediment that can be removed should be.

## Contraception after Childbirth

Contraception during the immediate post partum period may also cause some problems for sexual pleasure. Since there is really no way of knowing when each individual woman will begin to ovulate again, some form of contraception is recommended even for nursing mothers. Research has found that in spite of the centuries-old belief that nursing is an excellent form of birth control, nursing women can and do become pregnant.

Oral contraceptives are contraindicated for nursing mothers because the hormones in the pill can interrupt the normal balance needed for nursing. There is also the question of how much of the progesterone and estrgoen in the pill may be transferred to the baby through the mother's milk and what effect they may have on the infant. Healing time for fitting a diaphragm may be longer for the nursing mother because breast-feeding women tend to have more atrophy of the vaginal wall and decreased secretions, which make insertion of the diaphragm difficult and often painful.

Therefore, many nursing couples opt for prophylactics (condoms) as a method of contraception possibly for the first time in their lives together. The switch to condoms, while a very effective method of birth control if used every time there is sexual intercourse or used in conjunction with spermicidal foams or jellies, can be an adjustment. Couples must get used to stopping in the middle of a moment of passion to put the condom on. Women can learn to make the condom part of their foreplay by putting the condom on their husbands.

Sex with condoms feels different to both the man and the woman, increasing the difficulties in returning to normal sex. A nursing woman, who is poorly lubricated anyway, will probably find the use of a vaginal lubricant a necessity if her husband is wearing a condom. An appropriate spermicidal foam, cream, or jelly will make it more comfortable and add to the contraceptive value of the condom. Such lubricants allow the rubbery-feeling condom with its added friction to slide in comfortably. (Do not use Vaseline, which may eat holes in the condom fabric.)

If the condom is not to the couple's liking, foam or contraceptive jellies may be used alone. If the directions on the package are followed exactly, they can be a good form of contraception in themselves. The couple will probably find condoms, foam/jelly, or a combination of the two a necessity until the woman can be fitted for an IUD or diaphragm.

There is disagreement in the medical profession about how soon an IUD may be inserted after childbirth. Some doctors have exper-imented with inserting the IUD at the time of delivery, immediately after the placenta has been cleared away. This has resulted in a large number of spontaneous expulsions of the IUD by the uterus within a few days. There have also been a number of infections attributed to the early insertion of the IUD. Some doctors will insert it at the six-week checkup, but most perfer to wait until the woman has had her first period, which may take up to three months. (However, the doctor can give the woman some progesteron pills to take, which will induce a period and permit earlier insertion of the IUD if she is not breast-feeding.)

Fitting for a diaphragm may not be possible at the six-week checkup, either. It can take several months before a woman is at her permanent size.

Since the woman has not yet had a period, the rhythm method cannot be used for birth control. In addition, coitus interruptus, the withdrawal method of birth control, is not recommended. Withdrawal has always been a poor technique for both birth control and sexual pleasure and can be especially problematic for the woman during the unsettling physical.and emotional time of the post partum.

# What to Expect at the Six-Week Checkup

The six-week checkup has practically become synonymous with the resumption of sexual relations after childbirth, so it seems natural that many women would look forward to it, or anticipate some magical medical event. But what is it the doctor really does?

The six-week checkup normally involves a breast check, blood pressure test, and internal examination. During the internal exam, the doctor will check the healing of the episiotomy, whether the uterus and ovaries are back to normal, and the muscle tone of the vagina.

After the examination, the doctor will probably ask what form of birth control, if any, the couple intends to use. Some doctors may also offer some sexual counseling to prepare the woman for the physical or emotional changes she may encounter. However, in many cases it is the woman who must ask the doctor about sexual intercourse, pains, feelings she is having, or anything else that may be of concern. Doctors expect questions to let them know what areas are of concern to the patient. Don't be afraid to ask.

# The Experts Suggest

While there are genuine physical and some psychological problems associated with childbirth that are often at the root of sexual troubles, there are actions a couple may take to try to overcome the problem more quickly. Sexual therapists feel there are viable solutions to most of these problems, solutions that need not require therapy and can be effective from the first sexual encounter after childbirth to ease the entire situation to the point where there may be no problem at all.

Possibly the most important cause of sexual problems that can arise is the couple's reaction to the enforced abstinence period. Unfortunately, many couples interpret the ban on sexual intercourse to mean no sexual activity at all. Thus, by the end they are "climbing the walls." When they resume intercourse, they tend to forget the preliminaries that may previously have been important to their satisfaction and rush directly to intercourse. Of course, the woman is fatigued and possibly still recovering from the birth, so she may be slower to arouse; if there is little foreplay, she may not really be aroused enough to enjoy intercourse.

The resulting pain, discomfort, or just lack of satisfaction will not entice her to give up precious sleep the following night to try intercourse again, and a pattern of avoidance may begin.

It is important for all couples to remember that there are many levels to sex besides intercourse that could be enjoyed during the abstinence time. Cuddling, caressing, even orgasm without entry, oral sex, or manual manipulation of either or both. If couples are creative, then the return to intercourse will be, not a sudden jolt, but a natural, easy event.

There is no question that after the birth of a baby a woman is more tired for many weeks because her sleeping patterns are not the same. If she knows sexual intercourse may be unfulfilling because she never becomes fully aroused, she is liable to fall asleep and not wait for him or encourage him. If she anticipates a satisfying experience she will find ways to adjust. For most women "Satisfying" does not necessarily mean "orgasm." Many women are satisfied to have their affiliative needs met. Plenty of touching, caressing, and giving her the feeling that she is loved can be satisfactorily arousing for many.

Timing is a crucial factor.

"Luke was always upset about our sex life after the third child was born. He'd come home after seven, eat dinner, read or do some more work, then a eleven he'd expect me to be sexy," said Holly. "Usually I had long since fallen asleep—after all, I'd been chasing an infant, a toddler, and a seven-year-old around. I was pooped. Luke got more and more frustrated until he finally confronted me. We talked about it, and now we wake up about an hour before the kids and fool around then. It's great. I'm awake and we both enjoy it."

All the experts questioned on this subject recommended that each couple try to get away together without the baby as soon after the six-week checkup as possible. One commented: "The government should pass a law that it will subsidize a weekend vacation for all new parents when the baby is eight weeks old. That's how important it is."

Getting away can be revitalizing and cathartic. About one-quarter of the women interviewed had taken a weekend vacation with their husbands between the eighth and twenty-eighth week after the baby was born. Every one said it gave new life to her relationship with her husband and to their sexual lives. The women reported being able to relax and enjoy their husbands and their relationship, really getting back to sex as fully as before the pregnancy. They were also able to sleep at will and were relieved of direct worry about the child for the forty-eight hours. All said they returned with a new lease on their lives and marriage because they knew that things really were still good between them and that it was merely the day-to-day stress that was causing a temporary problem.

No woman should try to go from changing a messy diaper directly into bed with her husband for the purpose of making love. She should be able to take a little time in between to relax and feel like a woman and a lover. Even if that means stopping and soaking in a bubble bath for fifteen or twenty minutes, it will be time well spent. A nice hot, luxurious bath can make her feel feminine, and will relax muscles inside and out and help to reduce tension.

This exercise in relaxation can also be used as a joint time of sexual foreplay. Invite him in! If the bathtub is too small for two, try showering together.

Mood music, soft lights, candles, wine, and satin sheets weren't invented just for television and the movies. They can and should be used by couples who want make love in a romantic atmosphere. When two people who have just become new parents together get into bed, they should not be looking at each other as new parents, but as a couple who want to make love. It may take a little extra time and some planning, but the results will certainly be worth the effort!

# The Kegel Exercise

Anyone who has ever attended a childbirth training class has been told about the Kegel exercise. The Kegel is an internal exercise used to strengthen the vaginal muscles in preparation for delivery, but it is just as valuable an exercise after childbirth as before.

There is a subtle change in the vaginal muscles of all new mothers, both nursing and non-nursing, from the birth and ten weeks without intercourse. This difference is normally a loss of elasticity. Women may also find the vaginal opening may feel tighter because of lack of lubrication. The Kegel exercise can help and should be used by all new mothers, beginning as soon as they feel comfortable after the birth.

Men can Kegel, too. In fact, doing the Kegel exercise with the urinary and rectal muscles can help a man learn to stay erect longer and increase the intensity of ejaculation.

Doing Kegel exercises regularly can help lessen soreness from the stitches used to repair the episiotomy and can even help reduce pain from the hemorrhoids that may result from the sustained pushing during delivery. In addition, doing Kegels regularly can enhance the blood circulation in the perineum and promote more rapid healing and a more comfortable post partum.

Perhaps even more importantly, doing the Kegel exercise regularly can help to improve muscle tone in the vagina. This will help to speed the return to a satisfying experience during sexual intercourse. The vaginal muscles are stretched and weakened during childbirth.

Increasing the tone through the use of the Kegel exercise can help to make a woman more sensitive to sexual stimulation and firmer, which is more satisfying for both partners during intercourse.

Not all women find the Kegel helpful. Some reported that they did the Kegel several times a day as recommended and still had difficulty with sensitivity during sexual intercourse. However, since the exercise is simple and requires no special preparation, it is recommended by many doctors and childbirth instructors.

# How to Do the Kegel Exercise

The exercise consists of contracting and relaxing the muscles of the pelvic floor. To begin, one must identify the muscles in question. This is done by contracting as if holding back urination. Hold and relax. That action has exercised the muscles around the urethra.

Next, contract the muscles as if holding back a bowel movement. Hold and relax. The muscles around the anus were exercised with that effort.

Finally, contract the area around the vagina. Hold and relax.

To do the Kegel exercise, one must contract and then relax all three sets of muscles simultaneously.

The exercise may be done sitting in a chair, on the floor, lying down, or even standing up—and as often as you want.

Begin doing the Kegel exercise slowly. Contract the muscles in all three areas until the pelvic area almost lifts off the surface it is on. Hold it and then slowly release until the perineum is completely relaxed.

If you are doing the exercise correctly, the perineum will bulge out slightly as it does when passing a stool or urinating.

To test whether the exercise is being done properly try it while urinating. Spread the legs far apart, start urinating, then stop. If the urine flow will stop with the legs spread apart, you have done the exercise properly.

Since the Kegel exercise can be done in any position at any time of the day, fully clothed, many women suggested doing it when driving—

preferably when stopped at a long traffic light—or when cooking or watching television.

Every woman should do the Kegel exercise daily for the rest of her life because of its value in preserving the strength and health of her pelvic muscles.

# When Do You Need a Sex Therapist or Marriage Counselor?

When a couple's physical relationship plummets from exhilarating to practically nil after the baby is born, the couple may begin to wonder whether they need some form of counseling. It is difficult to say when a relationship has reached the point that sex therapy or marriage counseling is in order.

Most experts feel that it is a question of communication. When the couple feels there is a problem, but, no matter how much they talk about it, they can't change it, it is probably time to let an outsider try to help. If the problem is primarily sexual in nature, then someone trained in handling sexual interaction should probably be consulted.

Often a couple will find that very little counseling is necessary. Nancy and her husband consulted a sex therapist after having sexual relations only once in four months after the birth of their son. After only two sessions they realized their problems were not as deep-seated as they had imagined. They began to communicate more at home and found solutions on their own.

Many couples facing the problems of the post partum period find that a few sessions with a therapist can be a great help. Often just talking about the problem and understanding each other's feelings can be the key to resolving conflicts.

Being prepared for the sexual problems that can arise will not prevent them, but being aware that sexual problems are normal and not unique can minimize the emotional crisis that can result.

Although many women do not experience problems with sex after birth, every new mother (and couple) should be prepared for what might happen, just in case:

- Sexual intercourse may feel different from prepregnancy. The woman's body does experience some real physical changes that can affect the way intercourse feels.
- Some degree of discomfort or sensitivity during intercourse for at least the first few weeks after the six-week checkup is common.
- A reduced sex drive is common among new mothers. This effect may last as much as five or six months for non-nursing mothers or until after nursing ends for breast-feeding mothers.
- The biggest adjustment the couple will have to make will involve timing. Each couple must work to develop its own form of "planned spontaneity," finding the time of the day and style that is best for them.

The same may be true for the man involved. All of the postbirth problems that affect the woman, except the physical pain resulting directly from the delivery, may also affect her man's sexuality. He may find that intercourse feels different, which will take some adjustment. He may be suffering some fatigue from being awakened during the night and may not have his regular sex drive. He may be subject to the "distractors" such as listening to hear the baby breathe, stress from new responsibilities, or even job stress or money worries that may affect his sexuality. He may be working just as hard to adjust to fatherhood as she is to motherhood.

It may be the couple's sexual relationship that is the most obvious victim during the first months post partum. It is something that will take time, patience, and a great deal of caring to get to a level which they both enjoy once again. For some people therapy with a professional can help; for others time, communication, and working together will bring the answers.

CHAPTER SEVEN
# Working Mothers

It is not easy to be a working mother. Besides the stress of playing dual roles, the woman is constantly confronted with questions of the effect of her working on her children, her husband, and her own well-being, and of what is the proper balance among these elements. Deciding to return to work after the birth of a child should not be taken lightly. Every woman considering the choice should ask herself why she wants to work, whether this is really what she wants to do, and what the ramifications may be for her life and her loved ones.

Statistics show that in the United States today 40 percent of all married women with children (and husband present in the home) work.

Researchers at Seattle University studied 195 societies worldwide and found that in about half those societies the women returned to full work duties within two weeks. In only 12 percent did the women rest for more than two months. Few societies can afford to exempt women from making a regular contribution to the group workload for prolonged period of time as has become customary in the United States and other Western cultures.

Of course, because of the need for the women as workers, other societies have also organized and adapted to better incorporate mothers into the work force. Where babies cannot be taken to work with the mother, older women do the babysitting; women often nurse newborn infants as they work in the fields in agrarian cultures; and so forth, as part of accepted custom. Even in Western societies, when women in past generations worked, out of necessity, in mills, in sweatshops, or in the fields, there was usually an older family member to assist with child care. Be it a grandparent, aunt, or older child, someone stayed with the little ones when the mother went to work. Families were more extended and larger and members often lived within a few blocks of each other.

Today's working mother may be living hundreds of miles from any close relative, and teenage children attend high school or college and cannot be used for care of younger siblings. Therefore, today's working mother relies on paid strangers to care for her children. Some women opt for a live-in "nanny," or housekeeper; others have someone come to their homes during the day; and even more have come to count on day-care centers.

Such are some of the trials of being a working mother. Being a working woman with a husband and a home is hard enough; being one with a husband, a home and a child (or children) is a continual challenge. It is easy for the woman to begin to feel like a servant in her own home. She must establish some rules. She should set aside a time during each weekend when as much housework as can be done in, say, an hour or two will be done and not get upset about the rest. It is possible to vacuum an average apartment or small house, dust the rooms guests may see, clean the bathrooms so they are presentable and give the stove and kitchen counter a quick going over in two hours.

Older children must take responsibility for household chores. Valerie explained how her family of four kids survives two working parents: "Each of the older kids knows his or her duties. We never assigned any of them chores related to infant care, but each does have laundry, dusting, vacuuming, and table-clearing duties. They know they must do their part or they won't get privileges, so they do it." Of course, not all working mothers have children old enough to be a significant help. But even a six-year-old can do some light dusting, and Daddy can vacuum and shop without complaining.

Schedules will rarely be maintained, plans will regularly go awry. These are things with which a working mother must live. Even in the best situations there are too many variables, too many places where delays can occur, too many times the child's need or family interaction will take more time than expected, to keep to a schedule. It is wise to remember that, no matter what a critical mother-in-law may think, only a few generations ago human beings lived with dirt floors and without disinfectant cleaners, and managed to avoid extinction. A little dust on the window sill or a cobweb in the hallway will not spell the arrival of the plague to wipe out the entire family.

# The Husband's Role

How helpful the husband of a working mother will be may be a factor of his personality, but more often it reflects directly how he feels about her work. If he approves and encourages the job, for whatever reason, he is probably going to be more helpful with the child and household chores than if he resents his wife's role outside of the home. Some men want both the extra income her job provides and a wife at home, however. When the child comes and the husband still wants both, it is time for a renegotiation of their marriage pact. Otherwise, he may decide he doesn't want her working, while she has other plans. The woman may find there is great stress on her marriage with which she must deal quickly.

"My going back to work almost ended our marriage," said Mona. "He didn't want me to work, he wanted me to stay home and care for the baby and his home. He gave me absolutely no help at all. While I was on a constant treadmill, he flaunted his free time. We very nearly split."

Heather had a less serious problem with her husband. "He didn't want me to work, but I felt I needed to. He resented it alot. Every time he had to do something that a stay-at-home mother might do, he complained. But we worked it out. He helps out when he can now."

Times are changing and, with them, role models. Only a generation ago child care was women's work and women stayed at home to do their job. Today, more and more men in the middle socioeconomic bracket want to help with child care and want their wives to work. The reasons seem to be more than financial. Many men genuinely want to have maximum involvement in their children's lives and want their wives to feel fulfilled as more than just mothers.

"Jim teaches in a college, and he wanted me to go back to work as soon as I felt ready," said Valerie. "Right from the beginning he arranged his schedule so that he could take up some of the child care. He has to be on campus only three days a week, so the other two he takes care of the baby. He also is a pretty good cook, so he makes dinner very often. I couldn't work full-time and still have peace of mind if he weren't the way he is."

Besides the problem of child care, working mothers have to consider the way their work may affect their husbands and the probability that many home chores will be neglected. Despite the growing numbers of working mothers, the fact that women have, indeed, always worked and the tendency of some feminists to ignore the negative aspects of working outside the home, problems do exist for the working mother and probably have always existed for her. Whether she needs to work for financial reasons, intellectual stimulation, or another drive that is creating her work impetus, she has to deal with the problems and develop the needed balance within herself and her family the can make working outside the home combined with child bearing a fulfilling experience.

However, there is no superwoman. It is not easy for anyone to work a full day and then run home and care for children. And there is always the bottom-line issue hanging in her thoughts of whether her children are really her responsibility, a responsibility that she perhaps should not be passing on to someone else during working hours. The working mother will have to make adjustments, lose all her illusions, and cope with an overflowing cup of guilt to make working the experience she wants it to be.

# Taking the Plunge

The return to work is not easy. Women find they are torn. On the one hand, they like getting out and away from the child, but on the other they worry about the child and constantly feel guilty about leaving the child with someone else.

"It was very hard to leave the babies each time to go back to work when they were only two months old," said Dorian. "A mother always feels that she is irreplaceable. I worried a lot, but it was easier for me than for some women because I was leaving them with their father or my in-laws. Knowing someone who loves them is taking care of them has been a big help."

No matter who is watching the children, the first few times the child must be left by the mother are a time of great anxiety for her. This "separation anxiety" occurs for a number of reasons. Leaving a child, especially an infant, is a very emotional event. The mother is not only worried about the child's physical well-being and safety, but there are many feelings pulling at her.

The working mother knows there are things about her child's development she will miss. She may not be the one to hear the child's first word, or see his first step. Instead, a day-care director or maiden Aunt Minnie may get that pleasure—although in reality the parents will find that they get to experience many of the child's firsts, even if the child isn't with them all day. Also, there is the added pleasure of having paintings to display at home and listening to the child perform ABCs or songs months before stay-at-home children. The mother wants to be with this child and to share in its maturation, to be the one to cheer its achievements and give moral support, but realistically she knows that many times that just won't happen.

Probably, too, the first few times the mother leaves the child, the child will cry its head off. It has become used to one person, its mother, tending to its needs. Whether it be a tiny infant or a toddler, it is very dependent on its mother and she knows it. In fact, the older the child becomes, the more difficult this "abandonment" may become. A ten-month-old is much more aware of his mother's actual departure than a two-month-old. He may reach out his arms, yelling "Mommy, Mommy," with tears streaming down his face as she disappears out the door. This scene, which is acted out several times daily in day-care facilities all over the country, is emotionally wrenching for both mother and child, despite the casual front the mother may try to project for the world.

Women who do not need to work for the money, may give in to the emotional side and give up working after a few weeks or months. Ina reported that she went back to work when her daughter was two months old, but gave it up four months later when her mother-in-law could no longer babysit. "I just couldn't bear the idea of leaving her with just anyone. My mother-in-law was one thing, but when she left I realized I just didn't trust anyone else and that I really didn't want to miss any of the experiences I would lose if I were working. I also felt very protective. That child meant more to me than anything else in the world, and I felt I could do a better job than anyone else at caring for her. Thank goodness we didn't need my income to live," she said.

Whether to go back to work is probably one of the most difficult decisions a new mother will make in her life. Even if the family budget or her own inner drives and needs require that she work, making that decision and leaving the child can be painful for her.

"Before my daughter was born I was full of plans," said Randi. "I was going to do a lot of career-related travel and count on my mother to babysit for long periods of time. Once I had the child I forgot all about those plans. I settled on a part-time job in a college with day-care on the premises. Emotionally, I can't leave her for long periods of time, but this way I was working, using my mind, and still building something for a future date when she is in school and I can work longer hours. It's not ideal, but it is what I need now. How could I leave her? How could I not be there with her at least part of every day?"

# Guilt

"I had feelings of guilt when I went back to work. I still have them," said Vikki. "You have to have them."

There is no way for a working mother to escape feeling guilty about leaving her child (or children) in someone else's care while she works. As mothers, women feel they should always be there for their children, yet circumstances sometimes make that impossible.

Guilt can take two forms. The first is guilt simply from the fact that they must be apart from the child during the day. This is magnified every time the child becomes ill or gets a bruise. "If I had been there she wouldn't have cut her lip." "If I hadn't left him at the day-care he wouldn't have gotten chicken pox." These are not unusual feelings, irrational as they may be. A normal, healthy little child will fall and get hurt on occasion, even if Mommy is two feet away. Until medical science discovers a chicken pox vaccine, most children will contract that disease sometime. But that does not make it any easier for the mother. For every working mother there is that "what if" that makes her feel guilty every day. "What if Johnny needs me and I'm at work?" It will never go away.

If the woman's working is not really approved of by other family members, her guilt may be increased by the not-so-subtle comments by her mother or mother-in-law will make such as, "If he didn't go to day-care he wouldn't have so many colds."

The second side of guilt is that even as she feels guilty about leaving the child, she probably enjoys being away from him and in the company of adults with business responsibilities all day. So, not only does her child need her and she is not there, but in many ways she is *glad* she is not there. If that emotion doesn't make her feel doubly guilty, she is not human!

"I felt guilty because I left my daughter twenty hours per week to work," said Geraldine. "I thought of all the things I could be doing with her and how great that might be for her. Then her day-care closed down for two weeks and I was stuck at home with her. After three days, I thought I'd scream. She wanted my constant attention when she was awake. I couldn't make a phone call or sit down for a break. I hated it. Sure it makes me feel guilty, but I need my time away from her in order to make our time together better. It makes me feel *very* guilty, because I really love her, but I need to have my own time."

Heather agreed: "I love my baby. I had terrible separation anxiety when I went back to work and plenty of guilt, but I cannot be at home. If I stay at home I become a drab nothing of a person. I have a whole other thing I can do, and I have to go do it. As much as I love being with my son, I enjoy the feeling of getting out and going to work."

# Is There Harm to the Child?

Many women expressed anxiety over whether leaving their children every day would cause the children to have some deep psychological problems when they got older. Would they feel they had been unloved, abandoned, or rejected? Several questioned whether this reliance on outside care was just another form of a breakdown of the family unit that would come back to haunt them.

Since day-care centers are a product of the last decade or so, it is difficult to say with certainty what the long-range effects will be on day-care kids. What if a principal care giver is a housekeeper—one whose cultural background and values differ from the parents? What impact does this have on the children? Certainly there is the potential for problems. Children need adult role models, and many sociologists ask whether their babysitters will become their role models rather than their parents. Some people are concerned that the children will be totally adrift without any appropriate role models.

The women interviewed seemed to feel that their children were not being harmed by the experience and were, in fact, still using their parents as role models. "My daughter won't wear slacks to day-care because she always sees me in a skirt," said Geraldine. "It doesn't matter to her that the day-care lady always wears jeans. She definitely identifies with Mommy, which I love."

In fact, the studies that have been done to date comparing day-care children with children who stay at home with their mothers all day indicate that there is no problem. As of January 1983, there was not one study that indicated that being away from their mother all day was having an adverse effect on the children. In fact, most studies show that children who spend all or part of their day in babysitting environments where there are other children present learn to socialize more easily and adapt to school or nursery school more easily than their stay-at-home counterparts.

Of course, these studies are not conclusive and while they seem to indicate that separation from mother at an early age is not harmful to the child, no one will truly know the effects of a generation of working mothers with children in non-family care environments until the children become adults and can interact in society more fully.

# Working Mothering vs. Homemaking Mothering

One of the causes of guilt in working mothers is the myth perpetrated by the media and our society that the homemaker/mother spends a great deal of time doing things for and with her children. Somewhere in the psyche of every woman is the mythological image of a mother happily cutting out paper dolls, coloring Easter eggs, or baking cookies with the help of her immaculately clean, smiling, and cooperative child.

In reality, the homemaker/mother may never do any more of those activities than the working mother, and if she does try, it is certain the perfect little child will spill flour all over the kitchen or dye on the floor and the mother will vow never to try a second time. That is not to say that there aren't mothers who spend a great deal of time working with their children, because there are, but not every non-working mother, probably not even the majority, manages to spend quality time with her children. Remember, too, that some mothers who spend all their time at home are often stir crazy and would like to be able to get away from their kids from time to time. That feeling is not conducive to patience for teaching cookie baking to a two-year-old, or color-matching to a twelve-month-old.

It is not the length of time, but the quality of the time used that may make the difference. A working mother must work harder to make the time she is home good time for the children. She should try to arrange her time so she can completely devote an hour after dinner to the child—reading a story, playing with a favorite toy together. Of course, that isn't always easy. Work is tiring, dinner must be cooked, dishes washed, baby bathed and readied for bed, but the working mother must make that extra effort to find the time to enjoy her children and have them enjoy her.

# Working Mothers Suffer

No matter how well the child may be doing, working mothers usually suffer. They can spend much wasted time and effort flagellating themselves for not having more time for the child, or for not having more patience during the brief time they do have together, or for not having the time to prepare healthier meals, or for any one of a dozen other reasons they can contrive for causing themselves more guilt and pain.

Even women who enjoy working because of the intellectual stimulation or their need for a career and are not working because of an absolute need for the money, can find plenty of reasons to berate themselves for not spending more time and energy with their children. They also spend too much time concentrating on regrets they think they will have when the child grows up, and they'll look back and know they've missed things.

"I'm in a demanding job and I know I lose plenty of precious time with my daughter," said Nicole, "so I try to make up for it. Even on nights when I get home too late to have dinner with her I read to her before she goes to bed. I have to work because we need the extra income, but it bothers me a lot when our evenings don't go right. Sometimes I'm too tired to deal with her calmly, or in the morning I'm rushed and we end up fighting when I would rather leave her in a spirit of love. It is very, very difficult. There are many nights I go to bed almost in tears because I haven't had the relationship with her that I would like."

Mona explained how her working was very painful to her. "I felt as if I were constantly going in and out of different worlds. I was one person at work and another at home," she said. "I felt guilty about my daughter, and my mother-in-law and my husband nagged me about it. I finally quit. The money was helpful, but we can get by without it and I just couldn't take the stress and the guilt and all the pressures. It was difficult for me. I had to give up the idea of ever having the kind of career I had aspired to, and that was a painful decision. I was very torn. When my daughter was eight months old I finally quit working, but it has taken me two full years to come to terms with that decision. It was a very painful choice."

# A Working Mother's Day
# Takes Extraordinary Energy

A working mother holds four separate jobs: wife, mother, career woman, and housekeeper. Even when her husband is extremely cooperative, she will usually have the final authority and responsibility for the house and the child as well as her responsibilities at work and as a lover and helpmate to her husband.

The average working mother who works the standard nine-to-five job probably awakens around 6:00 A.M., showers, dresses, and then awakens the baby for breakfast. For the next forty minutes or so they eat and she, possibly with her husband's help, dresses and prepares the child for the day. Perhaps a lunchbox must be packed, and a bag with extra clothes and diapers. If the child doesn't feel like co-operating, there may be an argument or a physical struggle during which one of the parents will forceably dress the child or insist on some other specific behavior.

By 8:00 A.M., the child has been taken to the sitter, where mother goes through a farewell ritual which may include crying or other carrying on by the child. By the time she leaves the babysitter, she has already had at least one rough emotional confrontation either at home or at the sitter's. Now she must battle the rush-hour crowds and hype herself up for being pleasant, smiling, peppy, and efficient at work.

She puts in eight hours of physically and intellectually tiring work, perhaps dotted with calls to or from the sitter about the child's sniffles (or perhaps the child soiled all his clothes including the extras and another set must be gotten to the sitter somehow). Then she leaves for home.

She fights the rush hour, picks up the child, rushes home and tries to start dinner. As she attempts to throw a meal together, her child may be crying, tugging at her skirt for attention, or doing any one of a number of original new routines planned to drive Mommy wild.

"Why is it that every child is born with the instinctive knowledge of exactly the pitch at which to scream to drive his parents crazy?" asked one slightly drained mother.

Her husband arrives at home, he helps some by playing with the child, if he isn't too tired himself. Just as the woman finally puts dinner on the table, the child needs a diaper change. By the time the child is taken care of, the parents may very likely be sitting down to a cold dinner. After dinner, bedtime preparations for the child may begin.

Sometime between 7:00 and 8:00 P.M. the child is asleep and the mother can sit down for a minute. But only a minute, because there are still dinner dishes to do and perhaps a load of laundry. The house hasn't been vacuumed or dusted in a week, but she must wash her hair and iron a blouse for work tomorrow instead of cleaning.

About 10:00 she is finally in her nightgown and ready to sleep through the winter. She crawls into bed with one eye open and settles into a comfortable spot. Just as she is about to doze off she feels her husband's arm slipping around her waist and a gentle nibble at her ear. He wants to make love . . .

Weekends are spent at the supermarket and running other vital errands. Of course, the job is easier if one can afford domestic help, but not everyone can. More often, the working mother's day is similar to the scenario above and, with all the energy that requires, the woman will still berate herself for not keeping a cleaner house, or cooking more elaborate meals; or she'll become involved in volunteer work in the evening just to give herself some time away from the pressure. Of course, such excursions only add to the workload.

"We working women couldn't do it without understanding husbands," said Dorian. "Mine is exceptional and really does a lot of the work around the house and with the kids. But there is so much that has to be done."

# Babysitters

Clearly, the choice of who will take care of the children when mother is working is crucial to the entire arrangement. While some working women said that they felt a relative would make the best babysitter because of the emotional attachment with the baby, some feared a loss of privacy if they used certain kinswomen. Leigh commented that every time she has her mother babysit she comes home to rearranged furniture and drawer contents, which precipitates an argument dredging up assertiveness battles of her youth, something she would rather live without. Problems like Leigh's do arise when Grandma is the babysitter, so much so that one social worker commented that one should "never hire someone she won't feel free to fire."

For those who live far from family, or do not feel comfortable hiring family, there are several possibilities. One can hire someone to live in full-time or to come each morning and go home at night. Or the choice may be a licensed day-care center where there may be a large number of children, or a small babysitting service run by a woman out of her home. There are pros and cons to each.

Finding a live-in housekeeper/sitter is a major problem in many areas of the country. Some women reported followed up on ads in national newspapers from women in Ireland, Colombia, or other South American countries, or trying agencies specializing in "au pair" help from France. In many cases the potential employers pay the airfare as well as salary, room, and board. If the employee decides she is homesick after a few weeks, the airfare investment has been wasted.

Another problem is finding English-speaking housekeepers. "I decided not to import someone but to try to find one already here, so if something didn't click she'd have someplace to go," said Vikki. "But there were problems with language. My first housekeeper spoke Polish and the second Spanish. I had a third for a brief time who did speak English, but she sat on the phone most of the day with her family and friends, so I had to get rid of her."

Vikki had three sitters in just over two years. Nicole had two sitters in eight months. "The first one was from England, and she got homesick," she explained. "The second was from Ireland, and she lasted only a few weeks before she realized she shouldn't have left home, and quit."

Women who don't live-in but come to the home from early morning to late afternoon often last longer and cost less than live-ins, but they are also hard to find. Jessie was very lucky; she hired a practical nurse who stayed with her for five years as a sitter/housekeeper, working from 8:30 to 4:30 on weekdays. Of course there are sometimes problems with these sitters if both parents must work overtime on the same day. Often the sitters also have families and hungry husbands to feed and do not relish staying late. They are also expensive and may sometimes cost most of what the child's mother herself earns.

There is also the possibility, albeit rare, that one may hire a live-in or full-time sitter who abuses or neglects the child, is undependable or immature, displaying behavior patterns that would be potentially harmful to the child.

Licensed day-care centers vary greatly in quality. While the number of children per adult is regulated by state law (usually no more than four or five children per adult), some are better maintained than others or provide different services. Day-care supervisors are frequently trained in early childhood education; still, some may merely act as caretakers, while others may give children some nursery-school-type education, gymnastics, art, and music. The quality and quantity of cribs, cots, and even toys varies according to the amount of funding the center may have from the state or its parent organization (e.g. YWCA, Jewish center, church). Infants may not be as well-suited to a day-care center as an older child, who can run around and play with less direct supervision; and some day-care centers will not take children who are not toilet trained.

In recent years some women with young children who need to earn some money, but do not want to work out of the home, have started their own day-care services, taking care of four or five children in addition to their own. They may set up a room in the house with a couple of cribs or playpens. Many mothers find this smaller group arrangement completely satisfying, but it does have drawbacks. These women are rarely insured in case of accident or injury. They have their hands full watching five or six children and cannot always rush a sick or injured child to a doctor or emergency room since there is no one to watch the other children. Most of these women have no more training in child care than any other mother and offer no instruction or arts and crafts programs. They are simply adults watching the children, seeing that they are fed and napped and don't get into too much mischief.

Each possible choice should be investigated by the parents before a method of child care is decided upon. Quality of care, cost, type of care, and the pros and cons for the family situation should be carefully considered before coming to a decision.

# Arranging the Schedule
# (or, To Hell with The Household)

If both parents are going to work and baby is going to a babysitting service, schedules must be carefully planned. Since everyone must get up, dress, eat and get out at roughly the same time and still all get to work on time, cooperation is mandatory. Who showers first, who dresses and feeds the baby, who drops him off at the sitter this week, who picks him up, what can be precooked on Sunday and served during the week—all must be planned.

Somehow, no matter how hard the working mother may try to keep things on some kind of schedule, it never works. She arrives at the day-care center at 5:30, in a rush because Grandma is coming over after dinner and she wants to make everything look perfect, and her child is still in the midst of a late nap. The schedule will now be off by the half hour it will take to awaken the child and get him out of the center. Or, she arrives at the day-care center late, already wondering whether she can possibly have a decent dinner prepared when her husband gets home, and her fourteen-month-old has decided he doesn't want to leave the center. To prove it he has hidden his coat, and it is snowing outside. Grandma arrives to find the house not vacuumed or dusted, with laundry overflowing out of the laundry room and the breakfast dishes still in the sink. Or, Daddy discovers he is having hot dogs and beans for dinner for the third time that week.

Geraldine agreed. "Harold insists that I work. In part he likes the extra income, but also he genuinely wants me to have a career. As a result, we have divided up the child-care duties very carefully. He dresses her and gives her breakfast in the morning, while I shower and dress for work. I take her to day-care, pick her up and prepare dinner for all of us. After dinner he usually bathes her, and then we try to have time together as a family. Most of the time it works quite well. Of course there are days he has to stay late or be out of town, or I have a late meeting, and our schedule gets thrown off, but most of the time the duties are divided fairly well. We usually clean house together on the weekends. He vacuums, I polish, that sort of thing. It still isn't easy, because we are both so tired in the evenings, but we don't have any major conflicts where the child or home care are concerned."

In fact, some women commented that they didn't like the fact that their husbands wanted to be so helpful. They really felt certain things, like home and child care, were ultimately their responsibility, so they always left notes about exactly what to do when they were not around. But they also agreed that once their husbands felt confident in the jobs, they were probably ignoring the notes, which really is a good sign.

If a man objects strenuously to the woman's working or for some other reason will not participate in the child care/home care chores, she may find she should reevaluate working. Like Mona, she may find the income or even the personal satisfaction are not worth the exhaustion and mental anguish of going it alone. Mona finally gave up working and decided to go to graduate school part-time (on Saturdays, when her mother could babysit) in preparation for some point in the future when the children would be in school and she could work more easily.

# Not Doing Either Well

Many working mothers describe feeling as if they are living an almost schizophrenic existence. They feel they make a personality change as well as a role change when they come home from work and have to change back into mother and wife.

"It's a daily shock to the system," said Nicole. "I leave my private office carrying a briefcase full of important papers; I pick up the baby and go home to an apron, a stove, baby food, and the rest of the necessities. One minute I'm an executive, the next I'm wiping vomit off the floor. It's really mind-boggling."

Many also expressed doubts as to whether they were really doing their best at either task. "I know I'm not 100 percent committed to my job," said Bobbi. "If the baby needed me I'd leave work without a second thought, and I often find myself thinking about the baby during work. On the other hand, I'm not sure I really give my child the commitment she deserves. Am I a committed mother? I know I love my child like crazy, but I need more than just that. There is an unsettled feeling about being a working mother, at least for me. And constant questions. Am I giving her enough of myself? Am I messing up her psyche by leaving her every morning?

How can I explain that to someone who is not a working mother?" she asked. "It feels great to have a paycheck and be respected by peers on the job, and it also feels terrific to have those warm, loving little arms around your neck in a big hug. But I couldn't live with one without the other. Each fills different needs."

Not only can being a working mother make one feel that she is not totally committed to either job, but it may be difficult for her to get the jobs that she wants because she has a child. Working mothers may find they are held back professionally because they cannot work overtime or accept positions that require frequent travel. It is often difficult to be successful in a career if one cannot work more than a standard thirty-five- or forty-hour work week. The frustration will grow as others are promoted passed the working mother. It may be a very real problem for lawyers, doctors, stockbrokers, policewomen, women trying to succeed in the corporate structure, and many other working women.

Each woman must make her own decisions regarding work, decisions based on needs and value systems. The key is what each wants out of life for herself and her children, and no one can determine that for someone else.

Dorian said: "Remember that many, if not most, mothers work for the money. We could probably survive without the second paycheck, but not with the things we want for ourselves and our children. Not without worrying about 'What is such and such should happen and we needed cash?' So, much as we love our children, we adapt to running in two different directions at the same time. Sure, sometimes it feels as if you're going back and forth between two different worlds and you're not handling either very well, but that's the way life is."

## CHAPTER EIGHT
# Post Partum Depression

Experts have estimated that 80 percent of all women experience some form of post partum depression, today called an "adjustment disorder." Technically speaking, the essential feature of such disorders is a maladaptive reaction to an identifiable psychosocial stressor that occurs within a few months after the onset of the stressor (namely the birth of the baby). Post partum reactions fall into three categories: the "baby blues"; varying levels of mild or somewhat more severe depressions or anxiety attacks; and psychotic depressions. These reactions are usually of short duration and generally appear within the first six months after the birth. "Baby blues," in fact, normally occurs within the first ten days post partum.

Of the women who experience an adjustment disorder, roughly 2 percent develop the very serious psychotic reactions. These are debilitating, often trigger suicide attempts and are easily recognizable as illnesses by doctors. These infrequent cases are issues for psychiatrists and trained experts to handle and will not be discussed in any depth in this book. Instead, this chapter will concentrate on the mild or somewhat more severe reactions that strike a larger number of women, are difficult to recognize and, in fact, are sometimes ignored by doctors. These disorders can be quite upsetting to the woman and her family, yet are often vague and difficult to pinpoint.

Research into the causes of post partum depression and the relationship between "baby blues" and more severe forms of disorder is really in its infancy. Studies have been done at Stanford University, the University of Colorado, and other centers, but no conclusions have been drawn. Researchers have found, however, that women who experience anxiety and difficulty during pregnancy are more likely to have a more serious post partum depression, but this too is not a certainty. Some women are anxious during pregnancy but have no depression other than perhaps a day or two of the blues.

There is no question that some women do become quite strongly affected, either depressed or highly anxious, during the first post partum year. The symptoms and causes of the reaction are many (as alluded to in some measure in earlier chapters) and there may even be medical causes such as thyroid dysfunction, but whether the disorder can be predicted and prevented is highly questionable. The disorder commonly called post partum depression is triggered differently in different women and takes on different patterns of symptoms and severity.

It is a peculiar aspect of post partum adjustment disorder that it strikes when one would expect a woman to be the happiest, most fulfilled, and least depressed—after the joyous arrival of her child, an event she may have anticipated and desired for many years. New mothers who become depressed or anxious feel embarrassed and unworthy, increasing the problem and often delaying their finding help. In fact, the first year post partum may be the most stressful time in a woman's life, and she should not feel guilty about experiencing emotional ups and downs.

# The "Baby Blues"

The baby blues are experienced by a large percentage of women, who find themselves irritable, weepy, unable to sleep or concentrate on anything, and exhibit other symptoms of mild depression. Often baby blues occur while the mother is still in the hospital.

The "blues" usually pass in a few days, but the question many researchers have asked is whether a woman's susceptibility to the "blues" (or lack of susceptibility) has any relationship to her susceptibility to later, more severe, reactions. Research to date is inconclusive.

Since the "blues" can be very closely linked to the exhaustion of delivery, sudden hormonal changes, and very obvious emotional stimuli for the woman, it is a very distinct and common reaction of large numbers of women to the birth of the child. It is also something that women talk about and, therefore, are aware of and to some degree know they can expect. Thus, the onset of the blues is recognized even by the women themselves and is not a frightening experience, and it has no long-term effects on the women. Later depressions are much more mysterious, perplexing for the women and an unbalancing force that can disrupt the normal development of family closeness.

# Symptoms of Later Adjustment Disorder

Post partum depression can appear as late as five or six months after the child is born. These mild, moderate, or more severe reactions have many causes and many possible symptoms which gradually increase until they come together as a recognizable disorder. Physicians agree that these disorders, which have a severity somewhere between "baby blues" and psychotic depression, are of great concern because all too often the woman never consults her doctor, or the physician is not able to recognize the symptoms she describes until they worsen. As a result the woman may not be able to function well as a mother or wife and may suffer from a moderately severe depression for a long period of time.

These disorders may develop even in the best situations, where there is a father who actively participates in helping the mother with the baby or relatives nearby to support the couple emotionally. There is no way to predict who will suffer.

Just as each sufferer is different with different needs, so the symptoms may vary from woman to woman.

The symptoms of post partum adjustment disorders may include:

| | |
|---|---|
| headaches | bad dreams |
| back pains | feeling of being trapped |
| nervousness or shakiness | frequent feelings of confusion |
| dizziness or faintness | having to do things slowly to be sure |
| itching | they're right |
| trembling | feeling no one understands your situation |
| heart pounding or racing | feeling you can't get anything done |
| hot or cold spells | forgetfulness |
| feeling very tense or keyed up | asking others for directions on |
| stomach aches | simple things |
| butterflies in the stomach | feeling inferior to others |
| diarrhea | having to check and recheck things you do |
| constipation | difficulty making decisions |
| poor appetite | your mind goes blank |
| nausea | loss of interest in sex |
| fatigue | loss of interest in anything pleasurable |
| lack of energy | muscle soreness or stiffness |
| hypersensitivity to comments | suicidal thoughts |
| crying easily | feeling hopeless |
| uncontrolled temper outbursts | increased desire for alcoholic beverages |
| feeling sad | loneliness |
| ambivalence toward child | excessive guilt over things that go wrong |
| chest pains | excessive worrying |

Many of the symptoms are very similar to normal reactions to the confusing first weeks of parenthood, which makes them even more difficult to identify.

Certainly no one will experience all of these symptoms, or even most of them, and some people may have others to add to the list. The above are among the many possible symptoms, and their variety gives a clue as to why it is so difficult to diagnose and treat the problem.

It is estimated by experts that approximately 20 percent of all new mothers suffer from a mild to moderately severe post partum disorder during the first year after the child is born. Most of these women do not receive treatment for their problem, because they don't recognize the symptoms or because they are ashamed to seek help, feeling foolish not being able to cope with motherhood. Certainly having one or two of the possible symptoms may not indicate a depression, but any woman who suffers from a significant number of the symptoms would be wise to talk to her doctor.

# Causes

Most new mothers expect that the first months they spend with their new child will be the happiest of their lives. They will be fulfilled, loving, everything they have ever dreamed about will be theirs. Instead, after a few days, weeks, or months, they begin to feel inexplicably sad, they cry easily, they look forward to being away from the beloved child. They may ask themselves why they had a baby. Are they masochists? Each one thinks she is a freak, the only woman to feel unhappy or dissatisfied with a gorgeous newborn child. She therefore probably keeps it to herself, ashamed to admit that she is such a selfish, unloving person that she cannot comfortably share herself with her own child.

Of course she is not alone, and it is no wonder. There are plenty of reasons a woman could become depressed during the first post partum year. She would be justified in feeling a little down from any one of them, and, delivered in combination as they so often are, there should be no shame about feeling depressed and having to work it through. Fatigue, emotional drains, adjustments of body metabolism (of which hormones are a part) which can have a great effect on her physical comfort, are among the most easily identified reasons for the letdown. The problems of adjusting to motherhood, of adjusting as a couple to the new roles and lifestyles and the many feelings of inadequacy that can appear when trying to master the art of child care for the first time are central causes.

Previously working women may feel an enormous change in lifestyle in being at home all the time, watching soap operas, seemingly accomplishing very little except diaper changing. They develop a feeling of lack of achievement and of being unsuited to their new role. The feeling of being trapped or shut in with the child becomes depressing, especially when the excitement of having a new baby has worn off, when all the friends and relatives have seen the baby and are no longer popping in and life has developed a certain, dull routine that seems unending.

Even before the visitors stop coming, seeds of depression and insecurity may be sown when a new mother has to play second fiddle to her child. For nine months she was a center of attention, with in-laws, parents, and others fawning over her, jumping at her needs. Suddenly the focus of attention shifts to the baby.

On a deeper level, she may be overwhelmed by the amount of responsibility involved in being a parent. She had no way of preparing for the amount of pressure she would feel having an infant totally dependent upon her twenty-four hours a day. If she previously saw herself as a fairly "together" person who held down a responsible job, she may now be shell-shocked because she is so awed by the new responsibility and further upset because she finds herself unwilling to take it all upon herself. Instead she has turned to her husband, more than ever before in their relationship, to support and nuture her and to bear his share of the burden. Much as she wants and needs his help, she may also view it as a sign of weakness in herself which she does not understand or like.

She may be experiencing a delayed onset of maternal love for the child, a cause of enormous guilt and self-doubts. Or, she may feel guilty about any number of other reactions or things she has done, and the more depressed she feels the more the guilt may grow. She will actually feel guilty for becoming depressed at what seems like an inappropriate time in her life.

Other causes of a post partum disorder may include problems with nursing, depression after giving up nursing, worry over money problems since she is not working, self-perceived boringness because she does not get out in the world and have fascinating daily experiences, or exaggerated worry about the baby's health and well-being.

Many women experience problems with sex, which adds to their low self-esteem. They hate the way their bodies look with stretch marks and leftover fat here and there. They probably don't spend as much time a they used to on their own appearances.

Then there are all the "I shoulds." "I should be able to keep the house as spotless as before, but I don't." "I should be able to cater to both my husband and the baby, but I can't." "I should be eager for sex before bedtime, but I'm not." The list of "shoulds" is endless. Most women expect themselves to be perfect when it comes to balancing and completing normal household chores, but that is not always reasonable or possible for a woman who is concerned primarily with the care of a new baby. She now learns that superwoman/supermom does not exist, something she really did not know before. She had been under the illusion that her mother was supermom and never failed to accomplish anything, and that, not only would she too be supermom, but she'd do it even better than her mother. Reality has suddenly hit her. Her dream was unattainable, and her bubble has burst.

To top it all off, she may be overwhelmed by her own reaction. She never expected that she would succumb to those problems or that she might feel at all depressed, yet she does. That is the most difficult part of all. The depression begins to feed on itself: she feels unworthy because she was weak enough to become depressed.

The causes of post partum depression may be as varied as the women who experience it. Some women are more affected by their responsibilities with the baby, others by their lack of interest in sex, others by career dreams that may have disappeared. There is no certainty what will start the reaction, but a significant number of women do become depressed or anxious enough to need some help, be it counseling with their obstetrician, a visit to a psychologist, psychiatrist or family counselor, or the help of a post partum discussion group (which are now offered in some metropolitan areas).

Post partum depression, as it is popularly called, is not really a disease. It is an adjustment reaction or disorder caused by a real, chronic stress. Previous problems may act as catalysts for stronger reactions, but there are so many variables that no one can generalize or anticipate the reaction or degree of reaction. Therefore, there is a certain shock factor in finding one's self affected by the problem, a shock that adds to one's inability to handle it.

# Support Groups

Because so many women experience mild to moderately severe depression during the first post partum year, health-care professionals are becoming more and more aware of the need to offer services to help people adjust to parenthood.

Family counselors and social workers specializing in helping new families increasingly offer seminars for new parents or organize "support groups" where new parents can gather to discuss their feelings and problems. Women with friends who have had children during the same year frequently band together in what are commonly called "play groups." The children play while the women share their experiences and feelings, often in the presence of a doctor or counselor who volunteers to help them.

A recent study of support groups conducted at the University of Michigan indicates that there is good reason to believe that participating in group therapy or support sessions can significantly lessen the impact of adjusting to the new baby and thus help to prevent distressing post partum reactions.

Almost three-quarters of the individuals questioned in the Michigan study commented that recognizing the universality of their problems and being able to discuss them with others in the same position had given them reassurance. Almost half of the respondents said the groups had taught them not to doubt themselves and to have more self-confidence. Forty percent of the women in the study said they had had guilt over their feelings of boredom, being trapped, depression, and fatigue until they participated in support groups and heard that everyone else felt the same way.

Researchers feel that adjusting to parenting may be more difficult for the highly educated woman than for the less educated one and have found that educated women benefit more from support groups than their counterparts. A great deal of energy is required to integrate motherhood into one's identity as a woman. Talking with other women at the same stage in life may help a woman to clarify her own feelings and to express feelings about which she may be embarrassed or feel ashamed.

Feeling less than thrilled with one's situation, or one's status as a new mother is a very normal and natural reaction. Any woman who feels unhappy, insecure, or worried about herself as a woman, mother, or wife should certainly seek out a support group, a family seminar, or even a play group for sharing experiences and trying to avert more severe emotional reactions to the many problems and adjustments of the first post partum year. Too many women wait too long before seeking help, allowing their problem to grow and become more serious before they get help.

# When to See a Mental-Health Professional

When a woman has the feeling that she can no longer handle her daily life—in particular, the safe, healthful care of her baby—because she is suffering from a number of the symptoms listed earlier in this chapter, she should immediately contact her obstetrician or family doctor for an examination and consultation. During the appointment, she should try to be as frank and explicit as she can, so that the doctor will have a clear picture of her problem.

If after a thorough examination a physical cause for her problem is ruled out, then seeing a psychiatrist or psychologist might be necessary. It should not be an embarrassment to go to a psychiatrist or therapist. Many people consult mental-health professionals to help them cope when the pressures of the real world become too much to handle on their own.

## CHAPTER NINE
# When Baby Makes Four

In most families, the first born usually has a sibling within a few years—a totally new person with feelings, needs, and reactions entirely its own. It usually falls upon the mother to prepare the first child for this event and to cope with having two or more children pulling her in different directions once the new arrival is at home.

In addition, in today's world, where there is an increasing number of divorces and second families, the older child (or children) may often be considerably older than the baby and have only one parent in common.

Most of the women interviewed who had an older child considerably older than the baby felt that the new baby created no more work, because of the help received from the older child. Mothers dealing with younger children, however, spoke of an overload of duties and fatigue. Almost half the mothers with two children close in age said that two children were not double the work as reputed, but rather four times the work. Still, each experience was very individualized, depending greatly on the people, situation, and amount of thought put into preparing the older children.

# The Pregnant Mother

"I was lucky when I was pregnant with my second that there were several other mothers of young children in the neighborhood, so when my toddler daughter was outside playing with the children someone could help me watch her," said Ina. "There was no way I could have chased her when she ran from me, especially during the last couple of months."

A toddler or active four-year-old is hard to supervise when you are pregnant. Morning sickness may come even though breakfast must be prepared for the older child, legs may swell in spite of the need to be agile in pursuit of a foot-loose two-year-old. Mid-afternoon exhaustion may set in just as a three-year-old, refreshed from a nap, decides it is time to play on the backyard swings. In many ways, then, the second or third pregnancy may be more difficult and tiring for the mother. She probably will not get as much chance to rest or to take care of her own needs as she did during the first pregnancy. Her body and energy levels may simply not be on the same schedule as the bouncing, active child already in the house.

While the woman may find she has many concerns and anxieties during the first pregnancy, she will probably find she has just as many, or even more, during the second pregnancy—but they may be of a slightly different nature. Researchers have found that second-time mothers-to-be worry less about the delivery and slightly less about the health of the baby-to-be. However, they have a whole new set of concerns with which to deal.

Among the concerns are how to explain the pregnancy to the existing child and prepare him for the birth, dealing with the embarrassment that a much older child may have seeing his mother advertising her sexuality by becoming pregnant, convincing all her children that they will not be superseded by the new baby, and arranging child care while she is in the hospital.

There is no getting around the simple fact that the family unit and the lives of each member will be changed when the new baby comes, just as the first child rearranged the two-person relationship of its parents. No matter how hard the mother tries, her older child will now have to share his parents with the new sibling and will not be the center of the universe any longer. This has to be a shock, no matter how well it is handled. In many cases, the older child will react resentfully at first, or show hostility in some fashion. The woman knows she will be loving the newcomer and still trying to be as affectionate as ever with the older child. She will also be trying to give equal time to a demanding, crying baby and an older child whom she loves and who needs her reassurance that he is still very much loved by his parents.

To reduce the difficulties of the first weeks of adjustment, experts suggest preparing the child carefully for what is coming, taking into consideration the child's age and sense of time. (The older the child, the sooner he should be told. Young children have no sense of time and can hear the news much closer to the due date.) The child should be told of the impending birth and Mommy's hospital stay. Mothers should try to use a hospital that permits family visits. (Many hospitals have family rooms where young children can be brought to visit with Mommy and the new arrival, or the hospital may allow children into the mother's room for short visits.) Some experimentation has been done in which older siblings have been permitted to be present for the birth of the new baby in the home. However, watching a delivery may very well adversely affect a child's psychosexual development, because it will be very aware of the blood, mess, and Mommy's pain, so having a child present is probably not a good idea.

Researchers have found that the probability of disturbance over the birth of a sibling was greater the younger the age of the first child when the event occurred. Eighty-nine percent of children under three years of age had overtly negative reactions, but only 11 percent of those over six showed negative responses.

Even with a child over six, a mother may find that she has to extend herself beyond what she did the first few weeks after the first child was born, in order to keep the home front, and the children, in balance. To the older child, the baby represents a major source of competition for the affections not only of his parents, but of grandparents, aunts, uncles, and close family friends.

College of the Ouachitas

# Guilt over Sharing Yourself

Studies of family adjustments to second children have shown that in those cases where the older child reacts negatively to the coming of a sibling, the negative behavior is usually directed at the mother. Or, in simple terms, the first-born will do its best to make Mom feel as guilty as possible about "disrupting" its life by having a baby. Since the mother probably already feels guilty about having to divide herself between the children, the negative behavior of the child often has the desired effect on the parent—it increases her guilt and desire to somehow make it up to the first-born.

A mother often questions whether she is giving equally to all her children and whether any of them feels cheated. Many women worry about possible permanent damage to the children who feel "less loved" and their own abilities to keep expanding their love. In fact, human beings do not have a finite amount of love that must be divided up until it runs out. Love is unlimited, and love for children keeps expanding its bounds as the children arrive. The mother's ability to love her children and the problems of trying to spread herself among several at any given time are two different issues.

"The kids are all conscious of the shared attention," said Holly. "I know the littlest one is especially so. She is always hanging on to me. I deliberately registered the middle one in nursery school two mornings a week so I'd have time for the little one. It's real tough to give each one the attention they need. I have to find time to be with each alone."

Ruth agreed: "When my daughter was born I worried that I might shortchange my son, but that didn't happen. When I realized that my only chance to get out of the house many days was to drive him to after-school activities, I did it religiously—with the baby in her carseat. It was a treat for me to be out. The end result was that I looked for things to do with my son and he got more of my time than he had previously."

Heather found a similar case to be true: "The baby changed our lifestyle a lot. We began to stay home more, and then, of course, the older children got more of our time. So even though we were adding another child to give our attention to, at least during the first year when he slept a lot, all the kids benefited from more parental contact."

Even when the older children are excited about the prospect of having a baby brother or sister, when the reality of having less of Mommy's time and attention sets in, they are liable to react negatively through actions and words. Their mothers will, of course, be the one left feeling guilty, or at least responsible. She should not feel that way, because learning to share and realizing he is not the only person under the sun are facts of life important for a child to learn and to be able to handle. However, that wisdom doesn't make the exercise any easier for the parent.

# Dealing with the Reactions of a Young Child

An insightful new mother once suggested to her doctor that having a second child is exactly the same experience for the first child as any woman would have if her husband announced that he needed a second wife. Each would want to know why—hadn't they been good enough? It would be a most difficult adjustment. Since children under six generally are less accepting of their new siblings, the mother of a three-year-old—who would probably be active and a "handful" to manage anyway—can expect to have plenty of work during the first few months of her post partum, until the three-year-old accepts the newcomer.

Many first children revert to bed-wetting, forget toilet training, become more difficult to control, cry more often, or develop any one of a number of nervous habits at the arrival of the sibling. Generally, the behavior is aimed at getting Mommy's attention or upstaging the new baby in some manner.

Holly's son developed a nervous reaction to the birth of his youngest sister which gained him plenty of parental attention. "He started blinking his eyes constantly," explained Holly. "He was driving us crazy, so we took him to the eye doctor. After the doctor examined him he asked us how old the new baby was. We hadn't even told him there was a new baby. We answered that she was two months old, and he replied that she was the cause of the blinking. So I started giving my son more attention when the baby was napping and after she went to bed at night, and the blinking cleared up in a few weeks."

Many women respond that the reactions of the first-born to the newborn "got on their nerves," because they were tired and sensitive enough without the added pressure. The result was that the older child's reactions to the new baby were sometimes handled in a manner that made them worse until the mother began to realize what she was doing.

"I still feel guilty for the way I treated my daughter during the first few months after her brother was born. I was not understanding at all. She was torn emotionally. She wanted to love her brother and tried hard to be helpful, but she was also jealous. She developed a fever the first week—an emotional reaction. Then she gave us a lot of trouble about toilet training and I didn't handle it well at all," Nancy said.

Yet all the mothers added that mixed in with the negative reactions and the difficult adjustments on both sides were the good things. The older brother who became so protective of the new baby that he would not let anyone except his parents go near her, the three-year-old girl who emulated Mommy by putting her dolls to her breast to nurse, the older children who studied their new siblings from top to bottom to learn more about them.

Nancy recalled the reaction her two-and-half-year-old daughter had to her baby brother. The child was fascinated with the anatomical differences between boys and girls. "My daughter found having a little brother a very curious thing," Nancy laughed. "She couldn't get over the fact that he had a penis. She discussed it with everyone—at every opportunity."

# The Much Older Child

Since older children understand more of what is happening, their reactions are often more gratifying and in many ways easier for the mother to understand and handle than those of a younger child.

Problems that can arise with teenage children include the usual jealousies plus their embarrassment that their mother is pregnant, to them an announcement that their parents have sexual relations.

Estelle had three children, ages fourteen, twelve, and ten, when she became pregnant with the fourth. The children were very excited about her pregnancy. The ten-year-old was delighted that she would no longer be the baby and that she would have a little playmate. The twelve-year-old took to helping his mother cross the street by holding her arm. The oldest son would not let her carry large parcels or work too hard.

Yet there was that element of embarrassment on the part of the eldest. Estelle explained: "On the one hand he was very happy about the pregnancy and was only afraid he'd be too old to really be a brother to a much younger child, and on the other he was clearly embarrassed around his friends. I can remember picking him up one day after soccer practice. There was my son with all the other boy who were very athletic looking and towered over tiny me. My son was obviously embarrassed that he was being picked up by a very pregnant woman. He kind of wanted me to get lost.

"Since the baby came though, the oldest can't get enough of her. He feeds her, he changes her diapers, he rocks her to sleep. He peeks in first thing in the morning just to look at her. I'm sure they will have a very close relationship in spite of the age difference."

Heather reported that one of the biggest problems she had with her two teenage sons was that she couldn't get them to stop touching the baby. "The first person to finish dinner got to take care of the baby until everyone else was done," she said. "You never saw such speedy gulping down of meals!"

# Older Children from Previous Marriages

When the older children are not the product of the existing marriage, the mother may find she has special needs to attend to among the children, and more work in keeping the family functioning as a unit. Part of this effort should be made in preparation for the arrival of the new baby (often beginning before she is even pregnant), and the rest is a difficult set of adjustments that must be made after the child has arrived. There may be some sacrifices and decisions she must make that she never dreamed of before they began thinking about "a baby of their own."

Heather had two sons by a previous marriage, and her husband had two daughters by his first wife. She became pregnant a few months after their marriage. During the first year after the child was born, both boys and one of the girls lived with them.

"All the kids were excited about the baby," said Heather, "but we had more problems with the girls than the boys. Part of it was that this was my husband's only son. He was ecstatic about having a boy, and they knew it.

"I think the only crimp in my happiness was the way the two girls reacted. It was kind of a subtle manipulation rather than a direct attack, and it made things very difficult for me. I never knew where they stood and had to be on my guard for their attention-seeking, childish ploys all the time. They never directed their actions at the baby, only at me. In their eyes I was the stepmother who had caused all this."

Valerie had married a man with three children from a previous marriage who lived with them. She explained that she and her husband were particularly sensitive to the children's accepting her and a half sibling, so they waited several years and established a secure home in which the kids knew they were loved and knew where they stood before they had another child.

"Even so, problems arose. The eldest of the children, who was sixteen, became very concerned about her status in the family once the baby came. I guess it was about two weeks before my due date when she admitted her feelings and her fears of being neglected. Once the baby came and she realized things didn't change for her, she relaxed, and we haven't had any problems."

Valerie found that it helped never to insist upon baby care or any baby-related duties for the older children. "We didn't even insist that they babysit," said Valerie. "They have always done so willingly, but we never said, 'This will be your job.'"

Anna's husband had two teenaged children from a previous marriage who had just barely acccepted her when, ten months after her marriage, she gave them a half brother. "We've never had any problem," she said, "but of course they live with their mother, so we don't see them every day. They are fantastic with the baby and love to babysit, but I know if they lived with us things would be different. There would be a more direct threat."

# Becoming Attached to the Second Child

It is very natural for the feelings of attachment to the second child to come more slowly than they did with the first child. In part this is because the mystery and excitement of having a baby is reduced by the plain fact that it is not a new experience, so the woman is more matter-of-fact and casual in her attitude. The emotional impact is less.

There are other factors involved in the slow development of an attachment to a second child. It is more difficult to focus as totally on the second child as one did on the first, because there are more distractions (i.e., another child to watch). The mother's time must be apportioned between children and other tasks.

Other variables between the two children that were mentioned by mothers included the sex of the child (if they had one child, they invariably wanted the second to be of the other sex—if it wasn't, they were usually disappointed); the age spread (it was easier for many to accept the second child if the age difference was greater); and the child's personality. A small number of women did say that they loved the second more easily than the first. They attributed this to not being ready for the first, but wanting the second; and characteristics of the child (i.e., if the first was a colicky, cranky baby and the second was not).

The difficulty a second-time mother may have in developing an attachment to the second child are quite natural, but knowing that won't make her feel any less guilty when she had to deal with both children on a day-to-day basis. No mother should ever worry about the guilt she may feel; she must simply try to reduce it. Take a look at most family albums, and they will immediately reveal a striking difference. There will probably be dozens, if not hundreds, of pictures of the first child, but only a handful of the second, and half of those will be shots of both children. It is the normal way in which most parents react, as unequal or unfortunate as it may seem. A twenty-five-year-old second child arguing with her mother one day suddenly blurted out what had probably been a lifelong irritant. "You know you love her more," she yelled. "There are three pictures of her in the living room and only two of me—and one is *with* her."

Researchers from the University of Washington found that second children were touched less, looked at less, and played with less than first children. They found that mothers were more likely to leave second children with sitters and escape for the day once the older one was in school or to leave a second child alone watching television for longer periods of time, whereas the same mothers spent long hours teaching and playing with their first children.

Interestingly, women who had a delayed onset of maternal affection with the first child reported that they felt a strong attachment to the second child much sooner. They attributed that to being less nervous and being better prepared for parenthood.

"I felt an immediate attachment to my second child," said Nina. It took me weeks to accept the first, but I felt I loved the second right away. I think it was because I was more ready and felt more motherly the second time. The first time it was all kind of a shock."

# The Second Child Is Easy

Most women reported that taking care of an infant was much easier the second time around. While many agreed that they were more tired because they were caring for two children and getting less rest, they found the actual physical work easier, probably because they were now experienced. They had gone through their Masters and Ph.D. programs and were now ready for the job of baby care. In part it is easier, too, because the babies sense their mothers' lack of anxiety. Babies are very sensitive to the mood around them. If the mother is nervous, they will react by being more tense themselves. If the mother is more relaxed and assured, so is the baby.

In fact, second-time mothers call the pediatrician less frequently, spend less time feeding the baby (even nursing), are less nervous about baby care and less nervous about the child's health and safety, seem to expect less from the second child so they are not as watchful for every new deed, worry less about the child's playtime spills or what pebbles are going into its mouth, are more likely to take the infant out in all kinds of weather, are less easily flustered and are generally more relaxed.

"With two little ones, you don't have a lot of time to worry about the shine on the coffee table," said one mother of two preschoolers. "You're living with toys everywhere, so what difference does a little undiscovered dust make? I try to keep it livable. I don't poop myself out scrubbing and fussing the way I tried to do with the first."

# Each Child Is Different

Of course, some things cannot be anticipated, particularly the personality and routine of a new baby. Some mothers are quite unprepared for the inevitability of the second child's being a different person from the first. While the family probably goes through less trauma accepting the fourth member than the third because the husband-wife relationship has adjusted to the effect of children, many women expressed difficulty dealing with the fact that the second child had such different needs and responses from the first.

Mothers who had established certain patterns and routines with the first child were somewhat disturbed when the same techniques did not work with the newcomer. The difference created a job they had not expected, that of really seeing the infant as a person and studying him to learn what would suit him best.

They also found themselves doing the job of acclimating the children to each other. A younger child who is not controlled and is allowed to destroy the little clay figures made by the older will become a source of resentment for the older child, and jealousy and sibling rivalry will increase. Yet, the mothers asked, how much control will prevent problems with the second child but not make him feel like an also-ran, imprisoned in the crib, playpen, or highchair? This was another area that had to be mastered by trial and error. Each child had to learn its limits—new ones for the older child, who must be taught to be careful of the younger, and limits as part of basic learning for the younger child.

While baby care is much easier the second time around, there are more questions and challenges facing the mother that must be learned, dealt with, and adapted to the needs of each individual child. A proper job of mothering with a second child, then, would not involve just diapering, feeding, and plopping in front of the television or in the playpen. It really involves a whole set of complex interrelationships of individuals trying to find themselves, their place, and a balance with others around them.

# Breast-feeding the Second Child

The question of breast-feeding the second child has two elements: the actual nursing with all that entails, and nursing with another child around.

Most women agreed that nursing was better the second time. They were more prepared, more casual, and more aware of what nursing involved, therefore they got more out of it the second time. Women who were tense and unsure for several weeks the first time described nursing and talking on the phone or eating lunch simultaneously within a few days of the birth of the second.

Second-time nursing mothers were able to anticipate the possible pain of the first two weeks, were aware of how to prepare their nipples, knew how to deal with engorgement and knew how to keep the baby awake and nursing adequate amounts of milk. As a result, they found nursing more satisfying.

"Nursing the second child was much closer to the idealistic picture I had had before the first than nursing the first had been," said Ruth. "I loved it and nursed a lot longer."

None of the women interviewed in this survey had any qualms about being totally open about nursing with the older children around. The children watched the baby breast-feed, asked questions and took it as a perfectly natural fact of life. One mother reported using the time she nursed the baby to read to the older child. It was a quiet time that helped bring them all together as a family.

Certainly there can be problems. If the older child decides to flood the bathroom while the new baby is nursing and you are alone in the house, the feeding will be interrupted. Some older children may become jealous and may want to nurse, too. Experienced mothers recommended explaining to the child that he/she is now "grown up," but was nursed when he/she was a baby.

# Other Family Problems

To some this section may seem frivolous, but to those women who have had to deal with the problems described it may be right on the mark. "Other family" here describes those other older siblings: pets.

It is not unusual to find a couple giving up a dog or cat they have had for years, who was a surrogate child for them, because the pet could not adjust to the new rival. If there are older children who are attached to the pet, the parting is even more difficult. This is a highly emotional decision for some families. Even if the situation does not get to the point where the animal must be given away, pets often react by openly expressing their feelings about the child in ways that can genuinely throw off a mother's or a family's routine.

"I remember the first two days the baby was at home, our dog was impossible," said Geraldine. "She was *not* jealous, she was so excited she couldn't sit down. She's a Golden Retriever who loves children, and now she had a little person of her own. Every time I tried to nap, she woke me up. If the baby made a little grunt in her sleep, the dog would rush to get me and tug me to the crib in the baby's room. I was so exhausted by the end of the second day I could barely stand up."

Another mother told the story of her dog, who was rather spoiled by attention from the three older children before the new baby came. "When the baby was a few months old, the dog was outside in the yard and suddenly keeled over, paralyzed. The kids were hysterical, so we took him to the vet. The vet couldn't find anything wrong, but kept him for several days and charged us three hundred dollars. As suddenly as he got sick, he was well, and we took him home. The vet decided that the dog was simply looking for attention, the attention he had lost when the baby became the family pet. I've noticed since then that whenever the baby gets too much attention from the older kids, the dog begins to quiver all over."

Laura described the guilt she felt at not wanting her dog of twelve years around at all once the baby came. "I was so afraid she'd carry in some dirt or germ that would attack the baby that I barely looked at her or got near her for months," she explained. "And I felt terrible about it. She had been like our child, and here she was totally cut off from me."

Occasionally, too, a pet cannot accept the new child and nips, growls or scratches at it regularly. Unless a firm obedience course can stop the behavior, the pet will probably have to be given away.

The reaction a family pet has to a new child, or the realignment of family emotions including those surrounding the pet, can be an added problem for some women.

# Coping

The preceding pages outlined the many possible problems one can encounter with the second child. The women and experts interviewed suggested a number of ideas on how to cope with some of these possible pitfalls.

1. Give the older child a reason to accept the new baby, something tangible to make it worthwhile. For example, if he has been asking to stay up later to watch a particular TV show, let him and say it is because he is now a big boy. Make him feel as if he has received a promotion. Many parents use the gift of a bed, to replace the crib, as the child's incentive.

2. Don't be afraid to be a parent and assert your authority. Children need firm guidelines and want to hear their parents say 'no' because it means they care.

3. Don't overreact. Be observant of how you react to things your children do, and find your own standard of what you think is right. Don't hit unless the crime warrants it, and don't be afraid to apologize if you realize you overreacted.

4. Prepare the older children ahead of time for the birth, keeping in mind the child's age and ability to understand what is happening.

5. Wait until the first child is out of diapers and has become a human being you can talk to before having a second. This difference will be a help throughout the children's lives, not just in the beginning. One father

described how having children far apart was beneficial in his opinion: "I can remember very vividly one day when the third was an infant. My wife was preparing dinner and I was sitting in the kitchen holding the baby, playing Junior Scrabble with our middle girl and discussing Einstein with our eldest. All three children were happy and felt they were getting my attention, and because of the difference in their demands it wasn't that difficult."

6. Don't allow any visitor to show favoritism among children. Be sure guests talk to the older child before they get to see the baby. They should also be encouraged to bring a small gift for the older child.

7. Don't be afraid to go with your own gut feelings. You know your child better than anyone else, so do what seems right for your situation. Don't be afraid to be a little selfish sometimes. Don't let a jealous older child dissuade you from nursing, for example, if that is what you really want to do.

The best solution to most problems of multiple children is preparation. If the parents take extra care to see that possible causes of problems are avoided, there may be very little friction and a great deal of joy.

CHAPTER TEN
# The Single Mother

While this book has thus far concentrated on the woman's experience when the child's father is present, there are a growing number of mothers who are single during the first post partum year. These mothers have problems that differ from those of their counterparts. Even the issues facing single mothers may vary depending on whether they are single mothers by choice, by divorce, or by widowhood.

A single parent may have to handle all the work connected with the baby. A single mother knows that no matter how tired or even ill she may be, she is the only one there to answer her child's call. The single mother may experience feelings of guilt and selfishness when she does things for herself and have no one with whom to share the blissful moments of parenthood.

# Single by Choice

In today's society a new type of mother has joined the ranks of parents: the woman who, for whatever reason, has chosen to have a child without marrying, sometimes by artificial insemination. In contemporary America there is less of a stigma attached to unwed motherhood than in past generations. This has made it somewhat easier for these women to have their babies, keep them and be accepted on the job and in society as a whole.

The majority of these women are in their thirties and beginning to feel their childbearing time will soon be over. They decide they do not want to live a childless existence. Since adoption is often not a realistic alternative for single people, the only other choice is to have the baby themselves. They are eager to be mothers, want their babies and often plan for motherhood for several years before taking the big step.

Still, when these children are born they are unaware that Mommy is alone. They awaken at all hours, they cry, and they leave the single mother just as exhausted as her married counterpart—perhaps even more so, because unless she can afford long-term help or has a live-in friend or relative, she is the sole caretaker of the child.

In addition to the normal problems of the new mother, the single mother will soon develop other worries. She may wonder whether her child is developing too strong a dependency on her because she is the only constant adult present in the child's life. She may begin to question whether growing up without a male role model around the house will be good for her child's psychosexual development. She may begin to harbor guilt about whether this arrangement is totally "fair" to the child and whether it creates a reasonable environment for raising a child.

Many experts feel that one of the drawbacks of single mothering is that the mother and the child make an unnaturally large emotional commitment to each other. Such an environment may not be conducive to the growth of a well-adjusted child, something many mothers begin to question themselves as they watch the child grow from infancy.

Experts have other doubts about the advisability of the single-parent family for child development. There are many studies which indicate that girls who do not have a positive, loving relationship with a male adult as they grow up may have problems relating to their femininity as they mature. It is Daddy who teaches a girl that she is a girl. He is her first boyfriend, her first experience with the opposite sex. Little boys need a male role model, too. They need to see a man functioning day-to-day in a social environment, have an adult of the same sex present to help him understand his maleness, share interests that may not thrill his mother.

Many experts argue that by not having two live-in adults to watch, children do not learn communications skills in terms of interpersonal interaction, relationship compromises, and the like. They see only one adult who does things to please herself and the child. Studies have shown that these children grow up faster but are generally more immature and self-centered than children from two-parent families. They have problems in school in cognitive and intellectual functioning and often have difficulty controlling aggressive impulses. To counteract these potential problems, the single mother must act immediately to provide adequate support systems (to be discussed later in the chapter) for the child's development and their combined emotional well-being.

The mother herself may find she must face other issues which she may have considered but not fully anticipated prior to the birth. A major question is her social life. There are few men willing to get involved with a ready-made family. What if "Mr Right" comes along now and is not wild about the child? Or suppose the child cannot adjust to "Mr. Right?" And she now must have a babysitter to go out at all, even to a movie with friends. While she may have thought about this before becoming pregnant, the true impact of her decision will not hit home until the baby is several months old and she begins to want male companionship again.

Normal problems of all parents may become magnified, because she has no help in making decisions, no one to help her modify her response to a problem. (One cannot, after all, hear or see one's self or judge when one is over- or underreacting to something.) Also, she may start to worry very early about a guardian for the child should anything happen to her, and about how to pay for the child's education since it will be her sole responsibility.

However, several single mothers cited what they felt were advantages to being without a father with whom to share the child. They pointed to the fact that they had no one to argue with about child care, no resentments against the father like those harbored by many divorcees with children, no responsibility to make a man happy while caring for the child, no problems with in-laws, and no one demanding equal time with the child. "I think that adds up to fewer problems than married new mothers have," said Alice.

In spite of our more modern ways, there will still be people who are horrified at the idea of unwed motherhood. There may be coworkers who will shun the new mother when she most needs friends and support, neighbors who will treat her like a leper. Certainly the social rejection is lessening, but it is still there. How that may affect her child a few years down the road may be another of her inner concerns. Some parts of our society will still see the child as a bastard and punish the child for it. What will the mother do then? What happens when she or the child must fill out job applications, college forms, or other official paperwork that require the father's name? How will she respond? She must prepare early for these challenges.

Most single mothers must go back to work as soon as possible. A babysitter or a day-care center is a must, at some expense. The single mother may find it more difficult to get promotions or switch jobs if she tells potential employers that she cannot work late or travel for business. The fulfillment of having the child will probably help the mother to overcome many of the hurdles in her path, but single motherhood is not a simple matter and should be chosen only after much consideration, evaluation, and soul-searching by any woman.

# The Divorced Mother

Divorce during pregnancy and the first year post partum is becoming much more common. If there is any major problem in a marriage, the strain of childbirth and its aftermath can be the last straw. It is difficult enough for couples with good, solid marriages and healthy communications to adjust to all the stress on their relationship caused by the birth; a troubled marriage has a strong chance of breaking up.

The divorced new mother probably has the most difficult adjustment of any new mother. Not only does she have all the physical stress of all mothers and the responsibility of handling it alone, but she may be dealing with other guilt. She has not had time to adapt to the divorce before being thrust into motherhood. It is difficult for any divorced person not to wonder what he or she did wrong that caused the split. The woman may very well be feeling terribly inadequate as she learns to do all the motherly things that mythology call "womanly instinct" at the same time that she is questioning her value as a woman. Divorced mothers also often have the same financial problems as single mothers by choice, since child-support payments are not always reliable or adequate for the actual needs of the child.

In addition to her fatigue from child care, new adjustments as a mother, and other emotions she may be feeling, the divorced mother may also be angry at her ex-husband. That anger can cause problems with the child to be exaggerated in her mind. Imagine the dilemma of the divorced new mother who loves her baby, but has problems dealing with the fact that the child looks exactly like its father. It is perfectly normal for a recently divorced new mother to feel angry and trapped with "his kids." It is that kind of stress that can lead to child abuse or neglect in some cases.

Most commonly, divorced new mothers have difficulty accepting the situation. Many fall into patterns of denial, trying to convince themselves that the baby's father won't really leave. This denial plus the disapproval many divorcees with young children encounter (disapproval of the fact that someone with a rocky marriage would have a child, or that someone with such a young child wouldn't do everything to save the marriage and provide a two-parent home for the child) often add up to depression for the divorced new mother. The depression may be quite profound and long-lasting and have a major effect on the relationship that is developing between the mother and child and the mother's ability to care for the child properly. It is not unusual for a divorced new mother to need and seek counseling or therapy. In fact, most experts encourage these women to find professional counseling for however long they feel that it is needed. Counseling may be expensive, particularly for someone trying to make ends meet on alimony payments, however many ministers and rabbis are trained in family counseling and some churches and community groups have single-parent group-therapy sessions.

Of course, for some divorced mothers the child is a consolation. They can transfer much of the undirected affection they have to the child. That may be a plus for both or a negative if the woman becomes too emotionally bound to the child.

Another issue for the divorced mother is the question of her relationship with her former in-laws, who are also the child's grandparents. In some cases the divorce may not affect the friendship and the mother may continue to allow the child to visit the paternal grandparents and even use them for babysitters. However, in many cases her anger or their anger is too great. In those cases the child may never see those grandparents, which can be a great loss.

Divorce is never easy, but it is especially painful for a new mother. Certainly after a few years the divorced single mother will adjust, but the first year post partum may be the most difficult year in her life.

# The Widowed Mother

Unfortunately, life is never certain and people die. Thus, there are women who are widowed during pregnancy or the first post partum year. Each woman is different and may react quite differently as a mother in this very stressful situation. A woman may come to cherish the child even more as a part of her late husband. She may begin to idealize her deceased spouse and gain strength during the most difficult late-night vigils with the baby from her belief that he would have been a good father and that she must do her best for the child for him.

However, it is also very normal for the new widow to react quite differently in regard to her baby. She may go into a depression which leaves her unable to concentrate on the child, or even unable to properly care for the child for an indeterminate period of time. She may be so busy trying to reconstruct her own life that she does not have the emotional ability to devote a great deal of time to the child.

It can take up to two years to resolve one's grief, especially if death is a shock. During this time the new mother may have periods of denial of the situation, disorientation, depression, and resentment that her life turned out this way.

What most newly widowed new mothers need are people with whom to talk, yet many have found that they are in such pain they come to resent women with husbands, find it difficult to meet and talk with them and thus reject the natural support systems available to them in the community. "I was so destroyed by my husband's sudden death when our son was two months old that I lashed out at everything and everyone," said Kate. "It was months before I could relate to the child or begin to communicate with my friends again. I think that most of all I was angry, not at my husband, but that this had happened to me."

Anger is a very big issue for women left with young babies to raise. Anger at the situation, anger at the departed husband, anger at the child for being a burden—all may become all too real in those first months after the death. Guilt and self-hatred may also figure if there was anything she perceives she might have been able to do to prevent the death.

Any widow has many things to contend with, from her own grief to the estate, lawyers, funeral directors, and bills. For the widow with an infant the situation is all the more tragic, painful, and difficult. She will be depressed, unhappy, and exhausted from the rigors of child care. The most important thing any widow with a child can do to help herself is seek support groups. Whether she finds her help with a professional counselor, a minister, or an encounter group for widows, she must find the strength to seek the help for herself and the good of her child. National organizations such as the National Association of Widows (in New York City), the Compassionate Friends (Oak Brook, Illinois), or the Widowed Persons Service (Washington, D.C.) can help to find the nearest counseling center. Most clergymen will also know where help is available in their areas. Experts agree that it is essential that widows with young children find people to talk to so they can let the anger and negative feelings out and begin to concentrate on the positive, the mother-child relationship, and the future.

# Single by Choice and Gay

One group of individuals choosing to become single mothers today is gay women. Artificial insemination has made it possible for lesbians to conceive without having to become involved in a sexual relationship with a man.

If lesbian mothers live alone, their first year post partum will be much like that of any other single mother. They will face the fatigue, adjustments, boredom, and all the other aspects, both good and bad, that go with single parenthood.

Many lesbians who opt for children have a live-in lover who has agreed to the pregnancy. Undoubtedly if a new baby can break up a heterosexual marriage, it can do the same to a lesbian relationship. How long the lover will stay with a crying baby who is up at all hours depends as much on the strength of the relationship as it would in a marriage. It is no easier—in fact, it may be more difficult—to sustain a relationship with a lover who is unrelated to the child.

There are other questions that a sensitive, thinking lesbian mother must ask herself as the child begins to grow. Will the child be gay? Will it be confused by her sexual choices? Since there is every chance the child will not be gay, the mother may want to tone down her relationships to cause less confusion for the child until he or she is old enough to understand emotional preferences. If she does not have a live-in or steady lover, she may be more disposed to find one to reduce the confusion of many "friends" coming into the house. Or, she may want a live-in lover to leave so she can bring up the child independently. The many forces pulling at the lesbian mother make her decisions especially difficult in regard to both her own life and that of the child.

# Developing Support Systems

Being a single mother is no picnic. It is very challenging to the woman in terms of her own life and especially in regard to the child's physical and emotional well-being. While studies by experts indicate that single parenting is not the best situation for a child, the mother herself is under great stress, too. It is very difficult to bring up a child alone. Every single mother should examine her resources and find a support system that will be there for her.

There are community groups and clubs for single mothers or single parents that can provide some emotional backing and help by being social or group-therapy outlets. Parents Without Partners is a national group with branches in many large cities. A New York group, Single Mothers By Choice, is being emulated in many parts of the country, and there are many other choices available. Any women who needs this kind of support should contact her religious institution, YWCA, or county social services office for listings. The library may be a source for listings of meetings, as may a cable television community access channel. However, experts feel that the best source of support is the extended family—close friends and relatives.

Single mothers should endeavor to establish a good relationship with their own families and live as close as possible to a relative who will help with the child. Grandfathers make excellent male role models for children who lack fathers. Grandparents will sometimes babysit, as will aunts, uncles, cousins. Family members can also be good listeners or even offer solutions to child-care problems by drawing from their own experience.

If a family relationship is impossible, the next best thing would be for two single mothers to share a house or apartment and bring up their children together. This serves many purposes. The women can help each other, allowing each to have time away from home, and share basic expenses, and their children will have the opportunity to become very close to another adult.

While the male role model is still missing, children growing up in a home with two adults will learn many of the important lessons of communication, situational compromise, cooperation, and sharing that must happen every day in healthy, worthwhile relationships, be they friendships or marriages.

Single women can be excellent parents, but anyone who decides to go it alone should do so advisedly. It is an enormous task.

CHAPTER ELEVEN
# Getting Back in the Swing

After a few months, when the oohs and ahs are over and life with the new baby has begun to fall into a routine, most women begin to realize that their lives have become somewhat more restricted than they used to be. At the very time in their lives when they most need the support of other women and need the ability to get out and away from the overwhelming new responsibilities they have acquired, women generally find themselves the most isolated and unable to get away, because they are nervous about leaving their newborn with a babysitter.

They also can easily begin to feel trapped and unhappy with themselves. They feel stuck in a routine that is making them less interesting and therefore turning them into different people. Unfortunately many women don't deal well with this new perception of themselves and their lives, and it may take many months before they try to get out and become part of the world again.

Cassie described how she felt during the first year of motherhood: "I felt as if I had lost my identity. Everyone was expecting me to snap back into my old self, but I wasn't my old self anymore. My old self had been a fashion coordinator, an honors graduate from a respected college, an active, busy woman. Now I was a mother. I was stuck in a routine. I was constantly doing for others and never had time for myself. I had assumed a completely new role. How could I go back to being my old self when I wasn't that person any more? I was another person with new responsibilities and duties."

Part of the process of getting back out into the world and feeling like "yourself" again is very much involved with coming to grips with the new role of mother and the changing perceptions one has of one's self because of that role.

# Getting Yourself Together

"I can remember quite clearly the day I began to take hold of my life again, to mesh all my mixed feelings about motherhood and myself into my person," said Randi. "My daughter was about eight months old. I sat down to write a letter to a close friend from college, and suddenly, about the middle of the second paragraph, I realized that it had been a very long time since I had been able to think as clearly as I was that very moment about my life and what I wanted. I was immediately aware that the vague fogginess and depression I had been feeling were gone."

Randi began looking for things to do outside the home that same afternoon. She also began to send out resumes, which resulted in her obtaining a part-time job a few months later. Many women described a similar experience to Randi's. They could not explain why one day, when the baby was approaching its first birthday, they suddenly looked at themselves and realized they were ready to get out again, that their heads were suddenly clear.

Some said they felt it was because they had begun taking exercise classes, some linked it to reading specific books that helped them focus on themselves, some said it was because their sex drives had returned. Whatever the catalyst in the beginning of the recovery process, once they realized they were still okay the women immediately began doing many things which helped them to come to grips with the world in which they now had to function.

Shaking off the confusing emotions and vagueness that often accompany the first months of motherhood is similar to fighting a depression. The only way out is to force yourself, or have your mate force you, to do things a depressed person doesn't do, such as going to the beauty parlor or to a movie. The sooner you can motivate yourself to do things, the sooner you will snap back.

# Self Image

Perhaps the first sign that a woman has begun to come out of the shaky first months of motherhood is when she begins to become as concerned about herself and her physical appearance as she was prior to the birth. Along with this comes the desire to get her body back in shape. Of course, this must be approached with moderation and common sense. A crash starvation diet will probably only add to any residual depression and increase irritability. Any woman who is nursing should consider dieting only under the supervision of a doctor, to be sure she is still getting the proper nutrition to support both herself and her baby. Exercise requires modification, too. Overtaxing the body can lead to muscle injuries and fatigue.

Most women found that a carefully planned diet begun while taking an aerobic-exercise class, body-tone class, dance class or any one of the many exercise programs available today was exactly what they needed. Most women lauded the programs because being able to get out, exercise and meet other women (frequently other new mothers) made them feel especially good. Often, groups of women from an exercise class can be found meeting for coffee and conversation after the class, enabling them to compare notes about their experiences.

"I took an exercise class designed for post partum women," said Vikki. "We worked out for about an hour, then we sat and chatted about our babies and both the problems and the fun we were having. Everyone, including the instructor, had children under the age of 18 months, so it worked out very well."

Many women, in fact, find they become almost addicted to exercise classes, because they feel so good knowing they are working out their bodies. They continue going to classes for years after any post partum needs have passed.

Exercise records and videotapes are also available in many stores today. They are an excellent way for women who cannot find sitters to firm their bodies. A woman may use them alone or set up home exercise clubs for small groups of neighborhood women. The women can take turns watching the children while the others exercise together.

Some health clubs have discount rates for women who join together. Thus, two new mothers who joined together could alternate going to the club with watching both children and also take advantage of the lower rate.

Many doctors believe that exercise should be done before the baby is conceived. Starting an exercise program two years before becoming pregnant would be ideal for preparing for the stress of labor and delivery and the wear and tear of the early post partum. They feel that the tiring and physically draining months immediately following the birth of a child are not a time for the woman who hasn't exercised in years to begin further taxing her body with a strenuous exercise program.

However, it is only natural for women to be eager to flatten their tummies and tighten up some of the loose flesh that may appear on their hips and thighs as a result of pregnancy. Fitness experts, doctors, and women who have tried exercise programs suggested several exercises that are simple and effective. They can be found at the end of this chapter. (Of course, before starting any exercise program women should consult with their doctors, just in case there is a problem with the back, which would contraindicate exercising.)

Improving one's physical self-image, whether by diet, exercise, use of make-up, or all three is a vital component to getting back in the swing and coming to grips with one's new role and the realities of life.

# Removing Self-Imposed Problems

One of the first things a new mother must learn to do before she can really build up her self-esteeem and feel fully human again is to treat herself like a worthwhile person. That includes a whole range of things: eating properly, getting enough sleep, dieting, going to an exercise class, taking time away from the children, getting haircuts, facials, manicures—whatever makes her feel good about her physical appearance and well-being. But getting yourself together also require a kind of mental exercise—the development of perspective on what is really important and necessary, what can be put off, what can realistically be accomplished, and what the woman needs to stay in balance emotionally.

Many women impose rules, regulations, and limitations on themselves which do not help their recovery from the post partum period. For example, if there is a choice to be made between taking the child to the library toddlers' hour or going to her own aerobics class and she opts for the library because she has ordained that the child must come first no matter what her own personal needs, she has chosen to act in a self-imposed manner which answers to what she thinks a good mother "should" do, not what she as a mother and a person really wants to do. There are times when each of us must do things to meet the needs of others, but when our own needs are constantly made secondary to those of our children because that is what we think is "right," a good atmosphere for the mother to achieve a healthy mental balance has not been created.

Hillel, the great philosopher and teacher, wrote: "If I am not for myself, then who is for me? If I am only for myself then what am I and if not now, then when?" A little selfishness is okay, even from a mother, for if she doesn't stand up for her own needs now, who will? No one is required to spend all her time filling the demands of others.

The care of the child, the house, the job, and even one's relationship with one's mate must be put in perspective with the needs of the woman. Everyone is entitled to have personal needs and to have a chance to fulfill some of them. One of the points new mothers made most strongly in interviews was that they had to learn that they could not do for others constantly. Those who had achieved a happy balance and a healthy mental attitude all confessed that one day they had asserted "I need," and much to their surprise their partners were cooperative in helping them find a way to overcome the suffocation they had felt.

# You Do Have an Ally

The thing most women have in their favor, and which many fail to use, is that the father of the child can be an ally, a helpmate, and a sanity-saver. He can give her time off by caring for the child one or two evenings each week. He can relieve some of the other pressure on her by helping with household chores, shopping, and daily child-care chores.

The women interviewed for this book described mates who took care of the baby's breakfast when nursing was no longer involved, gave the child its evening bath, or agreed to maintain a regular weekly schedule by which he would be totally responsible for the children at least one night so that she would know she had that night of freedom to look forward to. Virtually every woman who successfully resumed working outside the home, whether part- or full-time, commented that she could not have done it without a totally cooperating and participating husband.

Even non-working mothers felt the importance of having the child's father do more than bring home a paycheck and occasionally occupy the child with play. One mother commented she makes it through long days chasing an active toddler because her husband takes care of the child's early morning needs, enabling the mother to sleep an hour or so after the child awakens.

A positive side effect of this division of child-care is that the children themselves seem to become equally attached to Mommy and Daddy. Daddy is no longer a semi-stranger who appears in the home right before bedtime and on weekends. He is an integral part of the child's life. Besides being excellent for the children, this alleviates some of the pressure on Mommy. She knows that she can leave the child with its father without coming home to hysteria on the child's part or panic on the father's.

Most women say, however, that they are still ultimately responsible for what goes on, which can be an irritant. Fathers may take credit for the good and blame mother's absences for anything bad that may happen, but the occasional problem does not outweigh the benefits of fatherly involvement in every aspect of the child's life. A mother should not allow herself to slip easily into routines that exclude the father.

Several women said they had been a little nervous about broaching the subject of being relieved one day a week so they could have some free time. Nancy said she had not been sure how her husband would react since he works a six-day week at his own business. She stalled for weeks, until the constant hassle of two children under three got the better of her. To her delight, it did not take much prodding for her husband to agree to rearrange his schedule so that he could give her time off from motherhood one afternoon each week. Leslie's physician husband agreed immediately that she could use his weekday off to her own purposes because he was eager to establish a closer relationship with the twins without Leslie's always being present. Jenny's and Geraldine's husbands allow them to sleep in most mornings by doing breakfast duty and are totally in charge of bath time each evening. "I don't even know what her bath routine is," laughed Geraldine. "If he is away on business, baths are very confusing because Mommy just doesn't do it right."

Jenny added: "The funny part has been that she became so close to Brad that she went through a period when she had separation anxiety from him everyday. She would cry when he went to work. I like it that she is very attached to him as well as to me."

# Helping Yourself

The first step toward getting back into circulation need not be a big leap. A small step forward will do nicely. A mother can begin by calling the doctor or local social service organizations in search of a post partum support group to join. These groups are gaining in popularity and are frequently sponsored by Y's, family counselors, or even groups of pediatricians or obstetricians at very low cost to the participants.

If a mother has friends who have children about the same age, she could try organizing a play group that meets for a few hours each week, enabling babies and mothers to socialize with their peers. One play group member said a pediatrician was willing to attend some of their meetings, free of charge, simply because they thought to call and ask him.

There are two kinds of play groups. The most common is very informal. New mothers hear about each other through friends and decide to meet weekly, alternating homes. The meetings are therapeutic in that the women compare problems and support each other. As the children get older and can really play with each other, the play groups expands its goals to provide structured play with all the mothers pitching in and lending whatever talents they may have in arts and crafts. Some groups have even worked out complicated schedules that allow the mothers to rotate so that each gets time free from the kids.

Becky described her play group as a wonderful experience. "We formed lasting friendships and still get together occasionally even though the kids are in nursery school now. We've even gotten together as couples for Saturday night parties. The play group was a terrific experience as a group activity and had many side benefits. For example, it gave each of us six other women who knew our kids, and the kids knew them and their homes, so if we had an emergency we knew we could find a secure place to leave the kids for a few hours."

A smaller percentage of play groups are more structured. They are established at family guidance clinics or by social workers. The women pay a moderate fee to meet under controlled circumstances with a trained group leader. Depending on the arrangement, the children may or may not be a part of the group activity. Connie found her structured play group to be "true therapy, which I needed. I look forward to it every week."

"My first move was to organize a babysitting co-op," said Erica. "I stood at the entrance to the neighborhood playground every afternoon and collared women with preschool children asking them to join." Babysitting co-ops are rapidly gaining popularity. They are small— usually no more than two dozen families—groups that get together to pool child-care. One mother will take care of another's child in exchange for similar services from the other family. Babysitting co-ops provide opportunities for socialization for parents and child. Having an adult, another parent, care for your child at no cost can certainly be preferable to hiring a teenaged babysitter at one to three dollars an hour.

Some babysitting co-ops are more structured than others, but an example of typical rules for a co-op are:

1. Each member will be given 20 hours worth of time tokens: 17 one-hour tokens and 12 quarter-hour tokens.

2. Sitting time should be calculated to the *next* quarter hour, e.g., 8 to 11:07 is 3¼ hours. Please pay your sitter from the beginning of the evening even if you do not go out immediately.

3. Daytime and evening sitting are paid at a "straight time" rate. Sitting after 1 A.M. will be paid as time-and-a-half.

4. The two families involved will privately decide whether the child goes to the sitter or the sitter goes to the child.

5. Children should be prepared for bed. No meals or baths, except by special arrangement, should be expected of the sitter.

6. Either parent may babysit.

7. If your child is ill, you must notify your sitter. Your sitter has the option of sitting or not. If she chooses not to sit, you must find a replacement yourself.

8. If there is a serious illness in the household of the sitter, she should call the people for whom she is sitting and tell them. The latter may prefer to find a replacement.

9. If you have more than 30 hours worth of tokens, do *not* accept sitting jobs. Do not get below 10 tokens for any length of time. If you find yourself in either of these situations much of the time, the babysitting co-op may not be what you need. Please evaluate your use of the co-op. If any members are not active as users or sitters, all members suffer.

10. If two members share one sitter, each pays the full rate. However, members should try to find their own sitters before resorting to this measure. The sitter must let each parent know in advance if she plans to sit for an extra child.

11. If a friend's child is to be sat for, the sitter should receive time-and-a-half. The sitter should be asked in advance if she minds sitting for the extra child. Such an arrangement should be made only when it is impossible for an outside babysitter to be hired by the other couple, as when out-of-town friends are staying with you.
12. When your supply of tokens is dwindling, let the secretary and other members know you'd like to sit.
13. At night, sitters should be accompanied home.
14. When you leave the co-op you *must* return 20 hours worth of tokens. If you are short of tokens, you should arrange to buy them from other members at the rate of $1.50 an hour or from the co-op treasury at the rate of $2.00 an hour. If you turn in extras, you are paid at the rate of $2.00 an hour.

If you are still nervous about leaving the child, you may want to invest in one of the inexpensive portable "beepers" like the ones used by doctors for the occasions when you use a sitter. Your nerves might be eased by knowing the sitter could contact you immediately in an emergency.

One of the biggest steps in helping one's self is to begin to find other new mothers to talk to. Women with many friends in the area have it much easier than those who have just moved into a new community or have mostly single or childless friends. The biggest help a mother can receive during the first post partum year is to be able to talk to other women, not so much for advice as simply to share experiences and to realize that all new mothers have similar problems, fears, and joys, and that no one is alone in the insecurities and changes that occur during the first year motherhood.

# Getting Out

Once one feels ready to get out again the question is "out where?" Women who worked full-time before having the baby and women who are new to a community may have no idea what is available in terms of cultural events and volunteers opportunities. In most urban and suburban areas of the country the possibilities for activities within a few miles of home are almost unlimited if one is willing to look for them.

Start by contacting your church, synagogue, local Y, or hospital. They would know where volunteers are needed and may even have listings fo women's organizations in your town. Women's groups and civic groups are always on the lookout for new members who can bring new ideas and skills into the organization.

The local library will have information on cultural programs such as films or concerts. Check the yellow or blue pages of the telephone directory for the addresses of museums, historical societies, the local amateur theater group, or whatever interests you.

Besides offering academic and degree programs, most colleges and universities today offer a wide range of noncredit courses, teaching a variety of skills (photography, sign language), crafts (pottery, painting), and even subjects of use in keeping household books. Your local high school may have an adult night school offering many of the same subjects one can take at the colleges, but for a lower fee.

Whatever a woman selects to do, the key is to find an adult activity providing contact with other adults and having nothing to do with your child.

Once the child is ready, taking advantage of some of the many "Mom and Tot" programs available at local Ys may be fun. There are Mom and Tot swim programs that begin when the children are as young as six months, toddler gymnastics for those who can walk steadily, and any number of other possibilities. The programs can be enjoyable and are often a good way to meet mothers with children the same age, but one must be careful not to join a class merely because it seems like a good thing for the child. Never do something for your child that you detest doing. Be choosy. Select only those activities that you find enjoyable and want to do with your child.

In most areas there are many possible activities. Besides the volunteer or the cultural or educational, there is no shortage of movies, tennis clubs, racquetball clubs, health and fitness centers, and places to jog in most parts of the United States. Getting out and finding enjoyable things to do is really a matter of looking. It's all there once you are ready to get going.

# Some Hints

There are ways a parent can organize the house to make leaving the child with a sitter easier and less anxiety-causing. The women interviewed suggested a few things that helped them to feel more comfortable leaving the child and more secure about their own control of household activities.

- Childproof everything. Put locks on all doors, cabinets, and drawers that might contain anything that could harm the child. Put safety covers on all electrical outlets, and gates at the top and bottom of all stairs. Carpeting all the floors is a safety measure, too, since the carpeting will cushion a child's falls.
- Use convenience products like disposable diapers and bottles if affordable. They do save time, and you will find sitters are more likely to change disposable diapers regularly than they are cloth diapers.
- Put the poison control number near all your phones in case your child decides to finish off half a bottle of baby aspirin or vitamins, or worse, when the sitter turns away for thirty seconds.
- Don't be afraid to ask sitters for references.

It is okay for a mother to get away from her child; in fact, it is essential for her mental and emotional health to have a break, time for herself, regularly. If she worked a paying job she would get weekends, vacations, and holiday time off. Motherhood is just as much a job, and the mother is entitled to regular breaks from her child-care routine.

# Exercises

The exercises recommended by corrective therapists, doctors, and many of the women interviewed which we have selected for this section can all be done at home, to musical accompaniment if that is preferred. They should be done on a mat or floor, not on a bed or mattress.

### 1. Bent-knee sit-ups for the upper abdomen

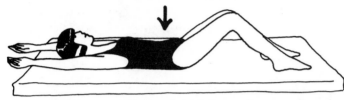

1: Lie down on your back with knees bent so that your heels are hip distance apart and 12 to 18 inches from your buttocks. Stretch your arms out straight behind your head.

2: Pull your navel to your back and slowly sit up. If you can't sit up completely, sit up until your hands reach your knees. (You can also place your feet under the front of a chair or sofa for added assistance until your abdominal muscles begin to regain their strength.)

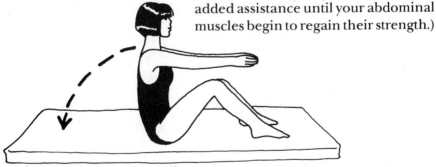

3: Slowly return to the supine position. Repeat this 10 times initially, building up to more.

## 2. Straight leg raise for lower abdomen

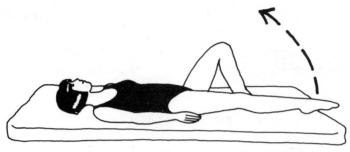

1: Lie on your back with one knee bent and the other leg straight.

2: Lift the straight leg to a 45 degree angle.

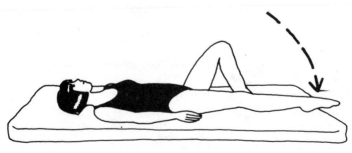

3: Return to the floor. Repeat this exercise 10 times for each leg, gradually building up to more as you feel ready.

### 3. Abdominal twist for the waist

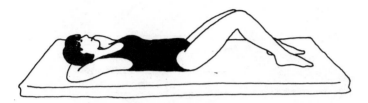

1: Lie on your back with both knees bent and feet on the floor. Place your hands behind your head.

2: Pull your navel toward your back. Lift your head and shoulders to sit up and bring your left elbow to your right knee, then right elbow to left knee. Do not bend the elbow forward to reach the knee. Keep the elbows back and twist at the waist. Repeat this exercise 10 times initially, more as you feel able.

### 4. Side leg raises for thighs

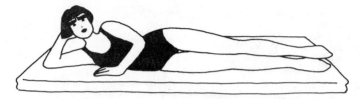

1:  Lie on your side. Keep the weight of your body forward so your top hip is being pushed forward. You may place your top hand on the floor in front of your chest for balance.

2:  Keeping your knees facing forward and your foot parallel to the ground, raise the top leg to a 45 degree angle. Keep the leg fully extended and contract all the leg muscles while lifting the leg.

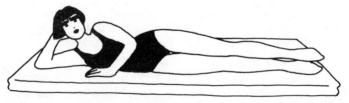

3:  Return to starting position. Repeat this exercise 10 times with each leg, building up gradually as you feel able.

### 5. Straight leg circles for thighs and hips

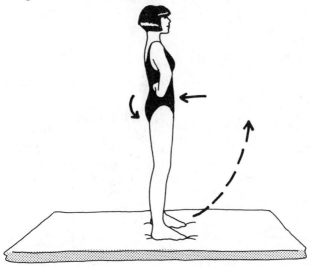

1: Stand up straight. Hold on to wall, chair or doorknob. Maintain good posture (pull in stomach and buttocks).

2: Keeping both legs straight, lift one leg up to 90 degrees.
3: Circle leg to left 5 times, then to right 5 times. Repeat with other leg.

### 6. Wall sit for thigh muscles

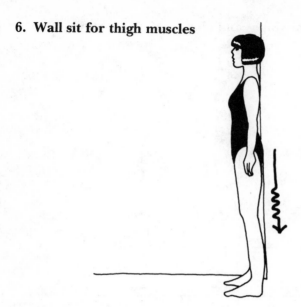

1: Put your back against the wall, slide down to a sitting position.

2: Make sure your thighs are parallel to the floor and your lower leg is parallel to the wall. Stay in this position for 20 seconds and then relax.

## 7. Hydrant for thighs and hips

1: Position yourself on hands and knees.

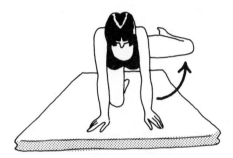

2: Balance on both hands and one knee while lifting the other knee out to the side so the knee comes toward your elbow.

3: Maintaining your thigh and lower leg in a position parallel to the floor, stretch the leg out straight.

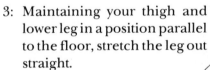

4: Fold leg back and then return to starting position. Repeat 10 times on each leg.

### 8. Hip roll and stretch

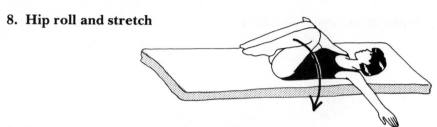

1: Lie on your back bringing both bent knees to your chest. Keep your hands extended out at shoulder height.

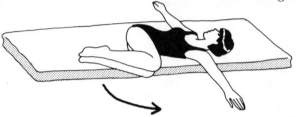

2: Roll your legs to one side and extend legs out.

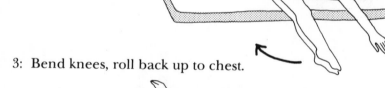

3: Bend knees, roll back up to chest.

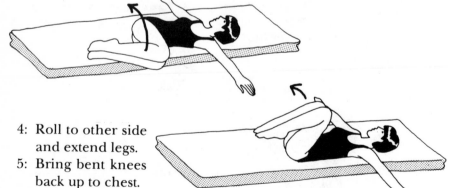

4: Roll to other side and extend legs.
5: Bring bent knees back up to chest.
6: Extend legs straight down to starting position. Repeat 10 times on each leg.

### 9. Pelvic tilt bridges for hips, thighs and derriére

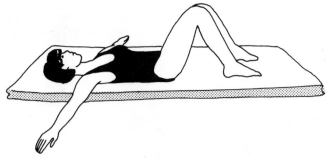

1: Lie on your back with your knees bent so your feet are hip distance apart and 12-18 inches from your buttocks.

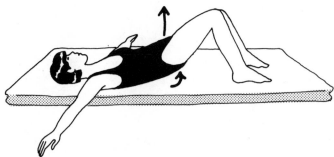

2: Tighten your buttocks and pull your navel to your back as you lift your hips off the floor. Keep lifting until your body is at a 45° angle from the floor with your shoulders and head remaining on the floor.

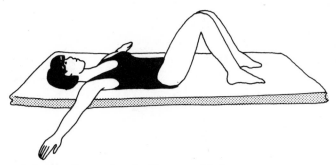

3: Return hips to floor slowly. Repeat 10 times.

CHAPTER TWELVE
# But It Really Is Wonderful

*"I don't know how you explain to people who have chosen not to have children that in spite of all the problems it is great to have children," said Erica. "They come to your house and the kids are tearing up the place, you're tearing your hair out, and it's very hard to explain why it's worth it.*

*"I remember one night we were at home playing backgammon with friends who don't have children. Our infant daughter was asleep, and our son, who was almost three at the time, was playing in his room before falling asleep. We were going on about how these friends should have a child because having kids was so fulfilling when we realized that our son had gotten very quiet. My husband went upstairs and found that he had somehow gotten into the medicine cabinet and made a mixture of baby powder and some ointments and had spread it on the hardwood floors of two bedrooms. We had just had them sanded and polished, and they were ruined. All the finish was stripped off.*

*"Our friends looked at us very skeptically, reaffirmed their vow never to have children and went home. Times like that I do feel about twice my age, but there are many, many good times that make up for it. Each child has its own special qualities. Each is an individual, and it is terribly exciting to watch them grow and learn from day to day."*

Why were many of the women being interviewed anticipating second children with great pleasure even as they spoke at length about how difficult and distressing first-time parenthood had been? How did motherhood really make them feel? Did it live up to their expectations?

In the long run, the answer is Yes, it did live up to prior expectations. But during those first twelve months many found that it was not at all what they had imagined. The shock of reality and the tangibility of all the negative incidents made them loom large and become the issues most discussed with others. However, most agreed that on an emotional level the positives far outweighed the negatives.

"How do you tell someone what it is like to hold your own tiny infant up against your body and to feel its soft skin and smell its own unique scent?" asked Dee. "I can tell you how it felt to be so exhausted I couldn't even speak, or how I burned the nipples the first time I tried to sterilize them, but to describe my overwhelming love and attachment to my daughter is much more difficult. That's inside, and it's sometimes very hard to verbalize while you're concentrating on learning the ropes of motherhood."

Becoming a mother is similar to a rite of passage. It involves pain, struggle, sacrifice, fear, and a unique maturational process. Yet the vast majority of women do pass the test and develop a sense of accomplishment along the way. In fact, in many primitive societies only adults who have children are considered responsible individuals. Those societies recognize better than our modern Western world that becoming a parent forces one to grow to full adulthood.

Each individual is solely responsible for how good a parent he or she is. Thus, as competence and ease in the role grows, so does a feeling of achievement and self-pride. The maturational process associated with being a parent can lead to stronger relationships with others. The ability to communicate and to be aware of the needs of others in the family can help in the long run to actually improve the relationship with the spouse, one's own parents, co-workers, and friends.

The first year may very well be difficult. Most women go into it with too little information. They have no training and an unrealistic picture of what will happen. They are unprepared for the amount of work, the exhaustion, the sexual and communication problems, and the myriad of other things that may show up during the first year post partum. Even if everything runs at an excellent level — the child is a good sleeper and eater, the spouse is understanding and shares the domestic work load — she may not have expected the fogginess. She may forget things, she may not be able to decide what to make for dinner for days on end, or she may just not exercise what she would consider to be her best judgment in many situations. That is all part of new motherhood, but a lack of realistic information may cause her to be taken by surprise and feel freakish for weeks or months.

One may ask why this seems to have become so much larger an issue in today's world than ever before. Certainly, the women of the 1980s are not the first to have babies. No one can say specifically, but there have been many changes in the role of women and in the role of the family in the twentieth century that may account for some of the reasons. As a pediatrician commented: "Mothers today demand too much of themselves. They are so much better educated than any generation of women to come before them, and they are very concerned about being the best mothers they can be. Perhaps they expect too much of themselves and the whole experience."

Certainly, women as a group have gone through immense changes in the last fifty years. The aftermath of World War I gave them the vote and the knowledge that they could competently replace men in the factories. The Depression put women to work to support families when men were laid off. During World War II women flew planes, drove ambulances and built war munitions. Then, while they were beginning to feel their strength, labor-saving devices arrived: the dishwasher, the refrigerator/freezer, the vacuum cleaner, baby formula, et cetera. By the 1950s, women were going on to higher education in proportionately similar numbers to men, and aspiring to be something other than elementary-school teachers or nurses.

By the 1960s, birth control was more reliable. The pill was widely recommended, and women could "have it all" — marriage, education, job, and sex without the constant fear of pregnancy. The message to an entire generation of women became: You can do everything you want. You can have a career, marriage and children.

Another phenomenon occurred simultaneously. People became more mobile, family members moving to various places throughout the country and even abroad. When a couple had a first child, there wasn't necessarily an extended family to help out. One grandmother explained: "It's different for new mothers today. I can't even relate to it. When my children were infants I had my whole family within a few blocks. If I was very tired or felt trapped or wanted to get out, I could always count on my mother, aunt, or brothers to come over and help. Even if they just played with the baby it was a help. I could shower or get something else done around the house. Women today who live miles from their families don't have that kind of opportunity. Also, in my day women rarely worked. They lived their lives expecting to be home with children even if they had some education, so we didn't miss what we had never expected to have."

The result of fifty years of growth is that women expect more from life than their predecessors but have fewer support relationships in their everyday lives. On the average they become mothers later than previous generations. More have college degrees and postgraduate degrees, and most have worked at least until marriage if not until giving birth. Of the women interviewed for this study only 8 percent had *never* worked.

Consequently, modern society has diminished the image of the woman at home. Being a stay-at-home mother is no longer respected. The glamor of the career woman has been extolled. In reality it is often easier for a women to have a career than to be a mother. It is easier to cope with something over which one can have some degree of control. Becoming a mother is a major step into a world of less control and more sacrifices and pitfalls. Some women enter motherhood with a fear of failure because of popular misconceptions about being a parent. If work is the challenge and motherhood the standard path that anyone can take, then to fail at motherhood could be devastating.

Why, then, does a woman have a second child even as she can vividly remember all the aggravation of the first? Because once the crisis has been passed and she no longer fears failure and has begun to mature, she realizes that it is motherhood that has given her the greatest sense of satisfaction in her life. All the corporate deals, court cases won, or books published do not give the sense of accomplishment that successful mothering creates. It is part of a continuum of life from generation to generation, an affirmation of creativity and growth.

In fact, three-quarters of the women interviewed said that after the first year of crisis passed, being a mother had made them feel very good about themselves. A large majority of the women felt that they had had unrealistic expectations of motherhood, a definite misconception of what it was like and how much work was involved, causing problems after the birth.

Nina said: "Raising children is harder than I ever thought it would be. I have a degree in child psychology, and it is still a guessing game for me. I just hope I am making the right choices. Yet, even so, it is such a tremendous experience. Having a baby grow inside you, giving birth. I don't know how you describe it to someone, but I'm glad I didn't miss the chance. It has definitely made me feel more like a woman."

"I was a grinning idiot," said Heather. "The baby was hard work, but I was so blissfully happy I walked around with a grin on my face for weeks. I hadn't expected to have the opportunity to have another child, but I did and it was wonderful."

Donna agreed: "Even as a childbirth instructor I did not expect the first months to be as exhausting and as difficult for our marriage as they were, but now that it is behind us I can say that having a baby fulfilled a kind of longing for me. I feel like more of a person since I had the baby and happier than I've ever been before."

As much as they complained about the rigors of motherhood, 80 percent of the women said they either felt sorry for childless women or felt superior to childless women. Laura explained: "I have tried to fight this perception, but I must admit that I feel a sense of superiority because I had this child. I'm not sure why. Maybe it's because I was afraid before the delivery and insecure about caring for the baby at first and I triumphed over those feelings. The experience of labor and delivery and learning to be a mother is so unique. Men can't do it. Some women, unfortunately, can't do it. Now that I've gone through it all I definitely feel wonderful about it — and myself."

Most of the women agreed that it is impossible to explain to someone who has not had the experience why, in spite of all the problems they described during their interviews, they really loved having a child and wanted to do it again. It is a totally emotional response, an intangible without basis in logic.

Perhaps, though, they are aided in the decision to have a second child by the fact that their expectations are different after the first experience. Expectations influence how we perceive situations. They are part of our subjective judgments of the quality of our lives and our satisfactions and dissatisfactions. When that first child comes, the vast majority of women expect a too easy, too wonderful, almost idealized life living "happily ever after" with husband, home, and cuddly, adorable baby. They are unprepared for the realities of round-the-clock feedings, diapers, colic, stress on their marriage and existing family relationships, lack of sex drive, or the many other problems that may arise. The first child is truly a shock and a learning experience.

But it does gradually change. The baby sleeps through the night, the mother adapts and begins to become quite professional in her new role, self-assurance and a renewed sexual drive generally begin to help solve the rest of the issues that can seem overwhelming during the first months if not the first full year of parenthood. When that happens, life beings to approach the earlier expectations, the bad things begin to fade from memory, and it is the best of the time that stays with most women. When they consider having another child, they are prepared for the rough times and eager for more of the good.

# Bibliography

Aldous, Joan, *Family Careers,* John Wiley & Sons, New York, 1978.

Alfonso, Dianne D., "Missing Pieces—A Study of Postpartum Feelings," *Birth and the Family Journal,* Vol. 4:4, Winter 1977, pp. 159-62.

Anderson, Sandra Van Dam, "Siblings at Birth: A Survey and Study," *Birth and the Family Journal, Vol 6:2, Summer 1979, pp. 80-87.*

Boston Women's Health Book Collective, *Our Bodies, Our Selves,* Simon and Schuster, New York, 1976.

Ciaramitaro, Barbara, *Help for Depressed Mothers,* The Charles Franklin Press, Edmunds, Washington, 1982.

Cronenwett, Linda R., "Elements and Outcome of a Postpartum Support Group Program," *Res. Nurs. Health,* 3(1), March 1980, pp. 33-41.

DeRosis, Helen A., M.D., and Victoria Y. Pellegrino, *The Book of Hope,* Bantam Books, New York, 1977.

Derthick, Nancy, "Sexuality in Pregnancy and the Puerperium," *Birth and the Family Journal,* Vol. 1:4, 1974, pp. 5-9.

Drogemueller, William, M.D., "Cold Sitz Baths for Relief of Postpartum Perineal Pain," *Clinical Obstetrics and Gynecology,* Vol. 23, No. 4, December 1980, Harper and Row, New York, pp. 1039-43.

Dunn, Judy, *Distress and Comfort,* Harvard University Press, Cambridge, Mass., 1977.

Eiger, Marvin, M.D., and Sally Wendkos Olds, *The Complete Book of Breastfeeding,* Bantam Books, New York, 1973.

Ewy, Donna and Rodger, *A Lamaze Guide: Preparation for Childbirth,* Signet Books, New York, 1976.

Friedland, Ronnie, and Carol Kort, eds., *The Mothers' Book,* Houghton Mifflin, Boston, 1981.

Fuller, William E., M.D., "Family Planning in the Postpartum Period," *Clinical Obstetrics and Gynecology,* Vol. 23, No. 4, December 1980, Harper and Row, pp. 1081-85.

Greenberg, Larrie W., M.D., et al., "Postpartum Education: A Pilot Study of Pediatrics and Maternal Perceptions," *Journal of Developmental and Behavioral Pediatrics,* 2(2), June 1981, pp. 44-48.

Greenberg, M., et al. "The Newborn's Impact on Parents' Marital and Sexual Relationship," *Medical Aspects of Human Sexuality,* 11(8), 1977, pp. 16-29.

Gruis, Marcia, "Beyond Maternity: Postpartum Concerns of Mothers," *MCN,* Vol. 2, No. 3, May/June 1977, pp. 182-88.

Hames, Cynthia Tomsu, "Sexual Needs and Interests of Postpartum Couples," *JOGN Nursing,* September/October 1980, pp. 313-15.

Inglis, Toni, "Postpartum Sexuality," *JOGN Nursing,* September/ October 1980, pp. 298-300.

Insel, Deborah, *Motherhood: Your First Twelve Months,* Acropolis Books, Washington, D.C., 1982.

Jennings, Betty, et al., "The Postpartum Period: After Confinement: The Fourth Trimester," *Clinical Obstetrics and Gynecology,* Vol 23, No. 4, December 1980, Harper and Row, pp. 1093-1103.

Jimenez, Marica Houdek, Ph.D., et al., "Activity and Work During Pregnancy and the Postpartum Period: A Cross-Cultural Study of 202 Societies," *American Journal of Obstetrics and Gynecology,* Vol. 135, No. 2, September 1979, pp. 171-76.

Jones, Freda A., M.D., et al., "Maternal Responsiveness of Primiparous Mothers During the Postpartum Period," *Pediatrics,* Vol. 65, No. 3, March 1980, pp 574-84.

Klemesrud, Judy, "Mothers Who Shift Back From Jobs to Home-making," *The New York Times,* January 19, 1983, p. C1.

Legg, Cecily, et al., "Reaction of Preschool Children to the Birth of a Sibling," *Child Psychology and Human Development,* Vol. 5 (1), Fall 1974, pp. 3-39.

Ludington-Hoe, Susan M., "Postpartum Development of Maternicity," *American Journal of Nursing,* July 1977, pp. 1171-74.

Macfarlane, Aidan, *The Psychology of Childbirth,* Harvard University Press, Cambridge, Mass., 1977.

Masters, William H., M.D., and Virginia E. Johnson, *Human Sexual Response,* Bantam Books, New York, 1980.

Monheit, Alan G., M.D., "The Puerperium: Anatomic and Physiologic Readjustments," *Clinical Obstetrics and Gynecology,* Vol. 23, No. 4, December 1980, Harper and Row, pp. 973-83.

Mostel, Stella, "Sexual Dysfunction in the Absent-Father Female," unpublished manuscript, p.35.

Murray, M.E., "Sexual Problems in Nursing Mothers," *Medical Aspects of Human Sexuality*, 10(10), 1976, pp. 75-76.

Paschall, Nancy, M.D., et al., "Personality Factors and Postpartum Adjustment," *Primary Care*, 3(4), December 1976, pp. 741-49.

Pryor, Karen, *Nursing Your Baby*, Harper and Row, New York, 1963.

Radl, Shirley L., *New Mother's Survival Guide*, American Baby Books, Wauatosa, Wisconsin, 1979.

Rich, Adrienne, *Of Woman Born*, Bantam Books, New York, 1977.

Richardson, A. Cullen, M.D., et al., "Decreasing Postpartum Sexual Abstinence Time," *American Journal of Obstetrics and Gynecology*, Vol. 126, No. 4, 1976, pp. 416-17.

Robson, Kay Mordecai, et al., "Delayed Onset of Maternal Affection After Childbirth," *British Journal of Psychiatry*, 136, 1980, pp. 347-53.

Schaffer, Rudolf, *Mothering*, Harvard University Press, Cambridge, Mass., 1977.

Sheehan, Franci, "Assessing Postpartum Adjustment," *JOGN Nursing*, January/February 1981, pp. 19-22.

Snyder, Charlene, et al., "New Findings About Mothers' Antenatal Expectations and Their Relationship to Infant Development," *MCN*, November/December 1979, Vol. 4, pp. 354-57.

Vandenburgh, Richard L., M.D., "Postpartum Depression," *Clinical Obstetrics and Gynecology*, Vol. 23, No. 4, December 1980, Harper and Row, pp. 1105-11.

Wagner, N.N., et al., "Pregnancy and Sexuality," *Medical Aspects of Human Sexuality*, (3), 1974, pp. 44-79.

Weiss, Joan Solomon, *Your Second Child: A Guide For Parents*, Summit Books, New York, 1981.

Withersty, David J., M.D., "Postpartum Emotional Disorders," *West Virginia Medical Journal*, 73(7), July 1977, pp. 149-50.

Yalom, Irvin D., M.D., et al. "Postpartum Blues Syndrome," *Arch. Gen. Psychiatry*, Vol. 18, January 1968, pp. 16-27.

Yannes, M.O., "Essential of Episiotomy Care," *Journal of Practical Nursing*, 25, 1975, pp. 21-34.

Zalar, M.K., "Sexual Counseling for Pregnant Couples," *Matern. Child Nursing Journal*, 1(3), May/June 1976, pp. 176-81.

GARLAND COUNTY
COMMUNITY COLLEGE
LIBRARY
Hot Springs, AR 71901